Ellen M Firebaugh

The Physician's Wife and the Things that Pertain to Her Life

Ellen M Firebaugh

The Physician's Wife and the Things that Pertain to Her Life

ISBN/EAN: 9783337054267

Printed in Europe, USA, Canada, Australia, Japan

Cover: Foto ©ninafisch / pixelio.de

More available books at **www.hansebooks.com**

THE PHYSICIAN'S WIFE

AND

THE THINGS THAT PERTAIN TO HER LIFE.

BY

ELLEN M. FIREBAUGH.

Illustrated with Forty-Four Photo-Engravings of Sketches from Life.

PHILADELPHIA, NEW YORK, CHICAGO:
THE F. A. DAVIS COMPANY, PUBLISHERS.
1900.

RESPECTFULLY AND AFFECTIONATELY

INSCRIBED

TO

Physicians' Wives in General

AND

TO THAT ONE IN PARTICULAR WHOSE GRACIOUS PEN
HAS DONE SO MUCH FOR CHILDHOOD, AND,
THROUGH CHILDHOOD, FOR ALL
THE WORLD—

MRS. FRANCES HODGSON BURNETT.

TO THE READER.

I TRUST I am not without that modesty becoming to a country doctor's wife, and so it may be well at the outset to offer a word of explanation as to how the present volume came into existence.

An invitation was extended to me last year, by the Æsculapian Society of the Wabash Valley, to read a paper before the society at its semi-annual meeting in October. The subject assigned me was "The Physician's Wife." It was a subject with which I was quite familiar, and the writing of the paper afforded me much pleasure, though the pleasure was necessarily lessened by the knowledge that many things that might be said, and ought to be said, must be omitted, lest it assume an interminable length. Without a thought that it would ever arrive at the dignity of print, the paper was read. It pleased the society, and it was at once voted that it be published in pamphlet form for distribution among its members, comprising, I believe, about one hundred and twenty-five physicians, in the States of Indiana and Illinois.

The pamphlet was duly circulated, and many kind and generous words in regard to it came to me from persons both in the profession and out of it, some going so far as to say that the little pamphlet should wear a more substantial dress and have a wider circulation. More than one voice within the profession said the subject was worthy of a more extended treatment, and urged me to write farther in regard to it. But, being a novice in literary work, I thought very little about the matter until, by chance, I came across a book in the office library entitled "The Physician Himself and the Things that Concern His Reputation and Success," written by an elegant and scholarly physician of Baltimore. (I draw my inference from the book alone, having no personal knowledge of the author.)

I saw that it was a large volume, and that it had reached at that time—1889—its ninth edition. Then the thought came, Why should not a small volume on "The Physician's Wife and the Things that Pertain to Her Life" find favor with the profession to the extent of one edition, at least? I decided then and there to make the experiment—to enlarge the original paper and launch it forth upon the world.

Then I took the big book home with me, and plunged into it with great gusto. I had read medical books before, and always, as I read, my thoughts had strayed off to the pious old gentleman who insisted on a young lady friend taking a ponderous religious treatise from his library home with her to read. When it came back he found this verse written on the fly-leaf:—

"If there should be another flood,
    For refuge hither fly;
Though all the world should be submerged,
    This book would still be dry."

But this book, being personal rather than technical, held my attention to the end, and was read with much pleasure and profit and—disappointment.

I had confidently expected, in a volume of

this character, to find some allusion to the physician's *wife* as a possible factor in his reputation and success, and kept out a watchful eye for the good things the author would say, that I might make a note of them and quote them in my own little volume, knowing that a volume of any kind progresses much faster and with less mental strain when one can make long and copious quotations of somebody else's ideas. But I got no help from the good doctor. I found that he had simply eliminated from his equation the unknown quantity, and proceeded to quicker work without it. (Men often make short work of dealing with their wives.) A lady, not a physician's wife, said to me not long ago, with exquisite candor, that she did think doctors had the silliest wives! Possibly the Baltimore physician was of the same opinion, and thought the less said about us the better. But perhaps I am doing the doctor injustice. It may be that he only forgot us; that would be quite natural. Or, it may be that he was too chivalrous to place us in the same category with *things* that pertain to the physician's reputation and success. Be that as it may, we are capable of forgiving and forgetting him; and I, for one, am capable of the greatest admiration for the skillful pen which could write a whole large volume on the physician himself and make no mention of his wife, knowing that my own pen, in one very small volume upon his wife, would have been hopelessly stranded could it not have made very frequent allusions to the physician, too.

That the little book has much of the first person in it is a matter of sincere regret to me, and I have pondered very earnestly over the question of "how to keep out of it"; but the fear—that must always beset the novice—lest I should not be able to find a publisher made me entirely too timid to cast about me among physicians' wives for material. I did not want to be known among my friends and acquaintances as the woman who wrote a book that could not find a publisher.

I have eagerly availed myself of any chance remark or of any incident related by a physician's wife in regard to her life, and I have brought from my memory whatever had found lodgment there from past conversations with physicians and their wives. In other instances I have drawn upon my own little experiences, believing that they bear sufficient resemblance to the little experiences of physicians' wives in general to make them enjoyable.

It is hardly necessary to say that this little volume relates especially to the wives of country doctors,—I believe that physicians practicing in towns and villages are so designated by their city brethren, and are quite willing to designate themselves so, not so much through any redundant modesty, perhaps, as through the knowledge that the word *country* has reference more to the region than to the doctor, and that the large cities are far from containing all the best-educated and best-equipped physicians.

But it may be that city physicians and their wives will not object to viewing from afar their country brethren and sisters, and getting a glimpse of vicissitudes of which their own experience has taught them nothing. And it may also be that there are city physicians who can look back to some "dim islet of time" that yet remains sunny in their remembrance, when youth and hope and a studious mind formed the largest part of their capital in some far-off town or village. And they may enjoy in retrospect what they could not now enjoy in prospect.

If the little book shall afford only a portion of the pleasure to those who read it that it has given me to write it, I shall not have written in vain.

E. M. F.

Robinson, Ill., May 5, 1893.

Note.—Since writing the above I have found that the author alluded to did say one honest and straightforward word in regard to the *meddling* wife of the doctor, for which I wish to give him credit, and which I most heartily indorse.

THE PHYSICIAN'S WIFE
AND THE
THINGS THAT PERTAIN TO HER LIFE.

ÆSCULAPIUS was the god of medicine. We know something of the marvelous powers imputed to him,—his skill in healing the most desperate diseases, and even, in one instance, of restoring the dead to life. Jupiter, enraged at his restoring to life one who had been torn in pieces by his own horses, killed him with a thunder-bolt; but he lived on in the hearts of the people, and in an old Roman city they erected to him a statue made of ivory and gold, which represented the god as seated on a throne of the same precious materials; and there, at his most famous shrine, every five years, games were celebrated in his honor.

In all the honors heaped upon Æsculapius

and in all the praises sung to his name his wife, it seems, had no share. Her name is nowhere mentioned. Perhaps in ancient times, as in the present, the mother was sometimes in eclipse, while the daughter shone forth that all the world might see. The fame of the daughter, Hygeia, the goddess of health, has come down through the centuries. Medicine has named one of its departments for her, and hence we have hygiene, the science of the preservation of health. So the daughter is held in great esteem, from which we may hope, perhaps, that some day the science which took its name from her will not be so much disregarded as it often is to-day. But the wife's name lies in eternal shadow.

Hippocrates was the "Father of Medicine." We know that he was born in the fifth century before Christ, that he came of a family of priest-physicians, inheriting all its traditions and prejudices, and yet was the first to cast superstition aside and to base the practice of medicine on the principles of inductive philosophy. But we may never know whether or not he had a wife to help him in his good work, for on that subject history is silent as the grave.

Galen, the most celebrated of the ancient medical writers, was born in the second century after Christ. He commenced the study of medicine when but a mere boy, and when he was only about 30 years old went to Rome, where he healed a celebrated philosopher and other persons of distinction, and soon, by his learning and unparalleled success as a physician, gained for himself the titles of "wonder-speaker" and "wonder-worker," thereby incurring the envy and the jealousy of his fellow-practitioners. (If Galen had lived in our own day, and had permitted himself to be called by any such title as the above, instead of incurring the envy and the jealousy of his professional brethren, he would have incurred their contempt and been dubbed, in all probability, a charlatan.) He was an old man when he died, but whether or not he died alone, whether or not a wife's hand ministered to his last wants, it is not given us to know.

We are very well acquainted with St. Luke,

the "beloved physician," through his gospel; but we know very little in regard to his personal history, and nothing whatever in regard to his  wife. Indeed, the wives of those far-off centuries seem to have made but little impress on their own or succeeding times. The name of one of them has come down to us with all its lustre still undimmed, but she was not a physician's wife; far from it. She was Xantippe, wife of the great philosopher of Athens. (And Socrates was not a physician; far from it. "No one," says his biographer, "ever knew of his doing or saying anything profane or unholy!")

I was looking into our Britannica not long ago,—that treasure-house of everything good which, with the impartiality of history, makes no mention of men or women until after they are dead. I wanted to see if there were any *good* points of Xantippe's character recorded. To my amazement she was not in there at all!

It may be that some cynical bachelor doctor reading these lines will say within himself that the reason I did not find her there is that she is not dead yet. But the genial married doctor will remind him that he is hardly in a position to draw conclusions of that kind, and that, living or dead, she was not and is not a physician's wife.

Not finding what I was in search of, and wishing to leave no leaf unturned to know the truth, I put that volume up, took down another, and turned to Socrates; and the thought came to me, as I turned the pages meditatively, that perhaps Xantippe, like Æsculapius, was only a myth and had never really had any existence at all, except in the imaginations of men,—a very pleasing but very fleeting illusion; for when I found the biography of the great philosopher, which covers nine large and closely-printed pages, I also found two lines in regard to his wife. It seems to me that therein may be found a fair and impartial estimate of the relative importance of the two in the world.

The simple fact is, too much has been made of the negative virtues of Xantippe, and it is a sad commentary on the masculine world that it is so. Perhaps where there is one man who has devoted some time to the study and comprehension of Socrates and the philosophy he taught, there are a hundred men who know something in a dim way of the shrewishness of his wife.

Thus does the evil that men and women do live after them; and it will always be so, because there will never be wanting in the world the spirit that perpetuates and keeps it alive,—unless, perchance, our bark may one day, in its cruisings upon the ocean of life, touch the shores of another Utopia, where we may land and breathe the breath of perfect life. But this is a slight digression. Let us return to the physician's wife.

We will pass over fifteen centuries of time, which brings us to the latter part of the sixteenth century and to the great name of William Harvey, the discoverer of the circulation of the blood.

It is said that the literature which has arisen on this great discovery would fill a library.

In the long and interesting account of his life we come across the brief statement that he married, in his youth, the daughter of a doctor who had been physician to Queen Elizabeth.

My patient search was at last rewarded: I had found the mention of a physician's wife! Though there may have been some doubt in my mind as to whether it was the daughter herself or her father's position that most attracted Harvey, still the wife was mentioned, which was of itself very encouraging.

Nearly two centuries later we come to another most illustrious name in the medical world, and, indeed, in the entire world. For Edward Jenner, the immortal discoverer of vaccination, was not for a country or an age, but for the world and for all time. His was a grandly benevolent life. His biographer says, "There can be little doubt that he would never have had the perseverance to carry through his great discovery had not his earnest benevolence pressed it on him as a duty to confer a great and permanent benefit on the whole human race."

It is very gratifying to read of such a physician that "in 1788 he married Catherine Kingscote, a union destined to form a most important element in his happiness."

So pleased was I to find so long and so significant a sentence in regard to a physician's wife that I read and re-read it and pondered upon it. Who knows? Perhaps the world might never have heard of Edward Jenner had it not been for the sweet counsel and sympathy of a wife who believed in him and in the ultimate success of his life-work!

Reading a little farther, I find that she died in 1815, and that he felt her loss very acutely. It was the signal for him to retire from public life. He never again left his native town (for Jenner was a country doctor), except for a day or two, as long as he lived.

It was worth her while to live to be enshrined at last so long and so lovingly within a great and tender heart.

We see from the instances given, which need not be multiplied, that times are greatly changed. Whereas history has seen fit to remain forever silent as to the wives of those physicians who lived and died centuries ago, yet, as we get nearer to our own times, we find the physician's wife sometimes mentioned, and occasionally accorded very honorable mention. And now, at the close of the nineteenth century, a printed record of any physician's life, be he eminent or obscure, would, perhaps, be considered incomplete without some reference to his wife and family.

It is the knowledge of this that has given me courage to write these pages without feeling over-presumptuous in so doing. For most physicians, like most other men, *have* wives, and it has long seemed to me that their position in the world is somewhat unique.

To the physician's wife who looks with attentive eyes on the little portion of the world which is her allotted sphere, and where her life is spent, many things must present themselves to which most wives, perhaps, are strangers; and while there will be, of course, much that is trivial and commonplace in this volume, it will not be forgotten that our lives are made up, for the most part, of trivial and commonplace things. Rarely do the grand and the heroic enter into the life of the average woman of these average times, and still more rarely does the world know of it when it does enter therein.

Perhaps in some prairie home, as humble as that of the peasant father of Joan of Arc, there lives as dauntless a spirit which hears as divine whisperings as those which fired with such wondrous enthusiasm the glorious Maid of France. But the time and opportunity for splendid action came to this Maid of Orleans which may never come to the brave spirit which dwells in the little home on the prairie. She will fight her battles, and fight them bravely, but so quietly the world will not herald her deeds. That is the difference.

But, standing in a medical library the other day and letting my eye range over the titles on the backs of the volumes, I reflected that there is not a physician's wife in all the world who has not one great advantage over Joan of Arc. She never learned to read or write, while the doctor's wife has every chance to become deeply and wonderfully learned, if she will only make use of her chances. For in the doctor's library, to which she has free access, are tomes and tomes, and in these tomes are polysyllables unending and *unspeakably* great.

And when some brother-physician comes down to dinner or tea, and the two doctors get talking together about some case, then

"Words of learned length and thundering sound
 Amaze the wondering rustics ranged around,"—

the wondering rustics, of course, being the doctor's wife and his sons and daughters.

And it may happen, sometimes, that the good wife gets deeply interested in the talk, and learns with humility the names of many of the parts of which these mortal frames are composed. And she may take down some of the big books and read an occasional chapter about it all. Merely to stand and gaze upon these volumes is to subdue her, and to take one in her hand and read in it is to fill her soul with awe.

Reader, when you find yourself going off into your accustomed doze on Sunday at church, do not blame the sermon or the atmosphere or any of the surroundings. One little muscle does it all, —the orbicularis palpebrarum. It simply closes the eyelid, and you cannot help it.

If you have a cornetist in your church you will please notice the action of a certain muscle in the side of his face as he blows his horn (presumably his own), and remember it is the buccinator muscle that expels the air which is transformed into musical tones.

The buccinator muscle is well developed in many persons besides cornetists. Especially is it developed in one branch of the medical profession, —a branch that receives no recognition from the profession, but much from an easily-hoodwinked laity.

It may not be hard to find any two members

of your choir bearing such an attitude toward each other that even a casual observer can see that it would please each of them to take a portion of the other's occipito-frontalis. Or if not so bad as that, the action of the corrugator supercilii can at least be frequently traced. The young gentlemen in your choir—yes, in all the world, in all ages of the world—have been fascinated and enthralled by one particular little muscle in the feminine face,—the orbicularis oris; and old men oftentimes are not exempt from admiration of the workings of that same muscle.

And now, gentle reader, when you feel a magnificent scorn and contempt for things or persons on this mundane sphere, do you know that one little muscle expresses it all and does it very accurately? And do you know that the name of that little muscle is the levator labii superioris alæquæ nasi?

I am reminded of Dr. Blimber and his sister Cornelia and their school, where poor little Paul Dombey was sent to improve his mind. Cornelia Blimber was "dry and sandy from digging in the graves of deceased languages." Their pupils were bright enough boys when they began their instruction; but by the time they were through, all of them were weak-minded and some of them were idiots. How strange, it seems to me, that there are not more idiotic doctors in the world!

Yes; a physician's wife learns many, many things.

For instance, if she see any one blush, she is able to account for it from a physiological stand-point. She knows that a nervous impulse has been started in his brain, which produces certain changes in the central nervous system, which in turn have an effect on the vasomotor fibres of the cervical sympathetic nerve. In consequence, the muscular walls of the arteries of the head and face relax, the arteries dilate, and the whole region becomes red. That is all blushing is. It is not hard to do, although there is a common belief that doctors do not do it easily; and since their wives are born to blush unseen and waste their sweetness on the desert air, it is not really of much use for them to blush either. At least, not for themselves; and I hope the time will be long in coming when they will be called upon to blush for their husbands.

No; rather let that palsied function within the doctor's own system resume its old and inconvenient sway. And that time will surely come when the conditions of his daily life are changed and softened. If such incapacity really exist, it is not the doctor who is responsible for it so much as his "environments."

One more item catches my eye just as I start to close the big book,—Gray's Anatomy. It is to the effect that when old age comes upon us our jaw-bone is found to be greatly reduced in size. One doctor sitting near was questioned as to the why and the wherefore of this, and he thought that it might be due to friction,—constant "jawing," etc. It may be true, but I cannot help reflecting aloud, as I close the volume and restore it to its place upon the shelf, that I shall never be in a position to verify his statement, since it was the *masculine* jaw-bone the great anatomist had reference to. The doctor thought I had a queer way of reasoning; but when I told him that woman was not specified in the item, and that when she is not specified man is always understood, he seemed to understand.

Physicians' wives have a motto. We have adopted it not from choice, but from necessity. It is "Watch and wait." The physician's wife, of all women, understands most fully what it means to watch and wait. No one outside the profession can ever know how many breakfasts and dinners and suppers have been spoiled in the waiting. No one except the doctor's wife or her house-maid can ever know how many dishes with their contents have been put into the oven to keep warm for the absent one who did not come.

Then it often happens that, since meal-time is long past and the doctor has not come, the wife makes up her mind that he has dined in the country again, and things are put back into the cupboard. When they have had time to get as cold as they can well get, he comes. And so it

is year in and year out. The doctor gets accustomed to it, his wife almost gets accustomed to it, and life goes on. Let her find what consolation she can in the assurance of the old poet that they also serve who only stand and wait.

The doctor's wife should often drive out with her husband as he goes on his business trips or on his errands of mercy or charity, as the case may be. It is good for her to leave household cares behind her once in awhile, and drive through fresh country lanes and fragrant woods. For every thoughtful person Nature holds her everlasting charms, and more frequent communion with her would make broader-minded and better women of us all. How delightful it is to get into the buggy and start for the country on a soft day in October,—lovely October, whose blue haze rests so tenderly upon the distant hills, and whose gorgeous robe is spread out upon the forest! Perhaps the doctor has two or three visits to make to-day, and his wife will go with him, feeling, as they drive along and drink in deep draughts of the delicious air, that life is all joy and beauty.

Just outside the town her eye falls upon a clump of trees far off to the right, and her thoughts go back in loving retrospection to days long gone by, when she, together with other little children, often wandered across the open prairie to these same trees and looked up longingly to where the wild-grape clusters shone, and she wonders if they shine there still. If it were not for the intervening fences she would ask the doctor to drive over there and let her sit for one brief moment in the old, familiar spot. But the fences are there, and they drive on. And now they are crossing a brook, and the October afternoon, by some magical process, is transformed into a June morning. A pair of small and dusty shoes are sitting on the bank, with a pair of small and dusty stockings, turned wrong side out, beside them, while a little girl stands on a flat stone in the brook and watches with rapt gaze the water go rippling and gurgling over her bare feet, and heaven lies all about her!

The scene changes, and the little girl, grown somewhat older now, sits, in the sunshine of a Sabbath morning, on the bank of that same brook, with another girl beside her still older than herself, and they are fishing! But the little girl's conscience is not at ease, and by and by she ventures to suggest to her companion that she does not feel quite right about fishing on Sunday, and that she never had done such a thing before. Her companion looks down from the far height of superior years and wisdom, and rejoins, disdainfully, "Huh! If you don't never do nothin' worse than fish on Sunday you'll git to heaven, shore."

This comforts the younger one a little, and she fishes away in silence. But soon a little uneasiness manifests itself again, which her companion is not slow to detect, and she puts a clincher to her former argument by saying, "Besides, you little goose, it ain't wicked to fish with a bent pin, because you'll not ketch nuthin'."

At this piece of logic, which much older and much more grammatical people have found good and plausible, the doctor's wife laughs aloud, and the doctor turns a surprised look upon her and asks her what she sees. She answers that she has only been seeing some pictures that "hang on memory's wall," and which had long been forgotten till the brook placed them once more within her mental vision.

They drive on, and after awhile the doctor points with his whip to a little house across the fields, and says, "There is the place where I am going "; then adds, after a moment of silence, " I hope the clover-huller will be there to-day."

" Clover-huller ? Why do you hope such a thing as that ? "

" Oh, nothing ; only I'd like you to see how it works."

Now, the doctor knows that his wife has no liking for nor comprehension of machines of any kind, and hence his words mystify her not a little. She turns them over in her mind, but before she can fathom their meaning and intent they are at their destination. The doctor alights, but his wife chooses to sit in the buggy in the sunshine, since she knows no one within. He goes in at the gate, and the dog goes growling off around the house. He has met the doctor before, and realizes very fully this time that discretion is the better part of valor. The lady can hear from where she sits a mighty scurrying inside, as of children being hastily ejected into the kitchen or some other apartment, and of chairs being pushed or jerked to their proper places. The doctor pauses at the open door and knocks lightly, and a very tall woman, in a very long and very blue apron, bids him "jist come on in."

Presently the wife is conscious that a battery of eyes is being leveled upon her. The heads of the smallest children fill up the panes of glass in the little window, while the heads of the larger ones fill the upper panes. The baby belongs in the upper row, since it is held up by one of the larger girls, and simultaneously they gaze at the unwonted spectacle. The lady in the carriage is in nowise disconcerted,—she is not even greatly amused; she knows that children living in the country do not see so many strangers as those living in the towns, and that it is a natural curiosity and interest they are manifesting; it is all right if they want to look at her, only she would like them to come out to the gate so she could talk to them. Her eyes rest for a moment upon the woods off to the east, so lovely in the autumn stillness, and then they fall upon a machine, resembling somewhat a threshing-machine, standing idle in the lot near by. This must be the clover-huller; but, since it is not at work to-day, she will not get to see how it works, as the doctor wished her to do. Then she wonders if the doctor is not about through with his call.

Suddenly the air is cleft by a contemptuous snort, and a woman's voice from the house swells out upon the stillness: "I've seed doctors before I ever seed *you;* and I've done a heap o' doctorin' myself, I'll let ye know that! I've buried three husbands and six children, an' I *doctered 'em all myself!*"

Then does a great light break in upon the mind of the doctor's wife, and she knows now that the clover-huller is not only there, but is at work.

After a little the doctor comes out, with a very broad smile illuminating his countenance, unties the horses, takes his seat, and they drive on.

"Do you encounter many clover-hullers in your rounds?" asks the wife.

The doctor laughs heartily, and says, "Not many. This one is an officious old woman of the neighborhood, who has a contempt for doctors in general and me in particular. Whenever I want to I can 'rile' her from the top of her head to the tips of her toes, and I want to pretty often. It is lots of fun to hear her when she gets a good start."

A drive of about two miles brings them to a large, comfortable-looking farmhouse, where they stop. It is growing a little chilly now, and, as the doctor's wife is acquainted here, she goes in with her husband. Everything is so clean and sweet and home-like. The good wife and her daughters, and the benevolent old farmer too, tell her they are glad she came. She knows they speak in no conventional spirit, but simply because they are glad; and she is glad she came, too. The doctor has gone into an adjoining room to look after the patient with a broken limb, and she chats with the family until he

comes back. When he comes out he tells them the limb is doing nicely, gets off a joke at the expense of the tall boy leaning against the mantel-piece, which causes him to shift from one foot to the other, and look a little embarrassed and the least bit resentful. Then the doctor spreads his hands before the cheerful blaze on the hearth, and says, "Well, we must be going." The busy physician finds little time to loiter or to linger.

They start homeward. The sun has been shorn of his rays now, and a big red ball hangs low in the west, more and more encroached upon by a purplish-gray bank hardly definable through the haze, until finally the red ball is swallowed up altogether. The gorgeous coloring of every way-side tree and bush is toned down by the fast-coming twilight. Soon the stars come twinkling out from their azure depths, and, as the eyes and the thoughts of the doctor's wife go wandering up into illimitable space, she makes her own the soliloquy of the shepherd-king of old: "When I consider thy heavens the work

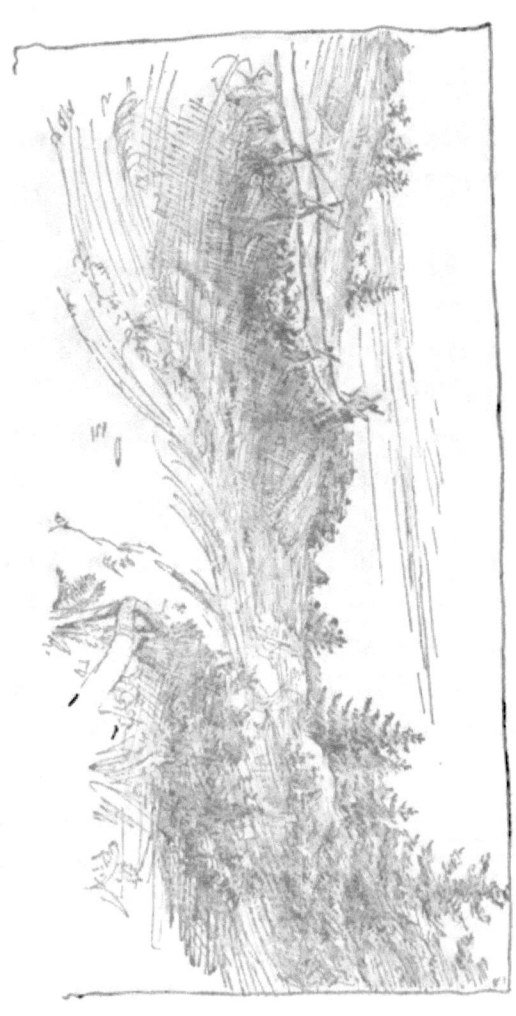

of thy fingers, the moon and the stars which thou hast ordained; what is man that thou art mindful of him?" What, indeed!

The horses' hoofs ring out with every quick stroke upon the highway; the fences fly behind them, by and by the lights of the town twinkle cheerily ahead, and the bells in the steeples are sounding their call to prayer.

They stop at their own door. And so ends one of many drives, and the doctor's wife is conscious that she is the better for it. She has been lifted up from the petty annoyances and distractions which are so often hers to serene heights where the soul loves to rest.

Doctor, when the weather is fine and the roads are good, do not wait for your wife to ask you now and then if you are going to the country to-day, and if it would be agreeable to you for her to accompany you. While you may answer "yes" with alacrity, it will still not be quite so pleasant to her as if the suggestion had come from you. You have learned, of course, in your daily life, that

> " Contentment is a richer gem
> Than sparkles in a diadem";

and you want her to know and feel it, too. Then, be assured that very little things like this go far toward teaching her the lesson.

It may well be that there is a physician's wife occasionally, especially if she be living in one of the smaller towns, who, thinking of the waiting, and the irregularities, and the annoyances to which her household is subjected, gets to feeling a little restless,—that her lot in life is circumscribed,—and, like Maud Muller, to longing for something better than she has known. But it may be, also,—and this I would have her remember well,—that, somewhere in the future, there awaits her a wider horizon, bringing with it care, and responsibility, and trouble which the old, quiet life never knew; when her thoughts will fly back to the little home, with all its little trials, as to a harbor safe and sweet. And she, too, will awaken to the knowledge—as very many have done before her—that ambition may oftentimes prove to be a glorious cheat.

There is a story of English provincial life which every physician, especially every young physician, and his wife should read together,—not superficially, as too many of our best stories are read, but very carefully. Not he who runs may read George Eliot profitably, but he who gives to her his most earnest attention. Most physicians and their wives have, doubtless, read "Middlemarch." Read it again. Mark the keen and fine analysis of the widely-different motives which actuate the lives of the ambitious young doctor and his ambitious young wife. Perhaps the ugly rock upon which their bark almost went down may be waiting to rear its head for you somewhere along the stream of your two blended lives. It is a powerful and pathetic picture which may find a parallel in many real lives. But, while our sympathies must be largely with Lydgate in his loftier and nobler ambition, we must, like the author, and like Lydgate, feel some sympathy with and pity for Rosamond, too,—the pity that one may always feel for a wrong and misguided life, which cannot recognize its own best happiness until that happiness has fled. Her ambitions were the best her nature was capable of; they seemed good and praiseworthy to her, and they, too, were shattered.

To me there is nothing in all fiction more pathetic than this: "Poor Rosamond's vagrant fancy had come back terribly scourged—meek enough to nestle under the old, despised shelter. And the shelter was still there: Lydgate had accepted his narrowed lot with sad resignation. He had chosen this fragile creature, and had taken the burden of her life upon his arms. He must walk as he could, carrying that burden pitifully." No husband and wife can live a happy and successful life when they have strongly-opposing hopes and ambitions. Then let us be one with our husbands in all their aspirations when we know them to be laudable, that the time may never come when we shall have to realize that they are carrying *the burden* of our lives upon them, though it should be carried ever so tenderly and pityingly.

Night at the doctor's house is different from what it is at other people's houses. Other people can retire and sleep in undisturbed repose, if their consciences are clear, while at the doctor's they never know what an hour may bring forth.

Here is a night at a busy doctor's in a busy season:—

The doctor, who has just returned from a long trip to the country, sits chatting with his wife, glad that work is ended and that he can retire to rest.

A knock at the door. He goes a little impatiently to open it. A voice from the darkness says,—

"I want some medicine for my girl."

"Who are you?"

Then does the voice grow big with astonishment and perhaps a little indignation. The owner of the voice steps a little nearer to the

light and says, "Great God! Don't you know
me?"

The heart of the doctor's wife sinks within
her. Her husband has made a mistake; he has
failed to recognize somebody of importance who
ought to have been recognized, and who evidently knows it. Some other doctor will do his
practice in the future,—so deeply into a man's
vanity can a little thing like that cut.

The man has stepped still farther forward
now, and she sees the doctor calmly look him
in the face and answer, curtly, "*No, I* don't
know you."

The wife breathes more easily now, and an
explanatory and even meek voice says,—

"W'y, I'm Josh Boyles."

"Where do you live?"

"Way down in the other end of town."

"What is the matter with the girl,—how is
she sick?"

"Well, she's got a pain in her stummick."

"What's she been eating?"

"W'y—I dunno—bread—an' m'lasses—I
guess that's about all."

The doctor believes in the efficacy of medicine, of course, and gives it to him,—it is of no use to charge for it; but he believes also in the efficacy of some other things that it is not his province to prescribe, and which it would be wholly useless to prescribe if it were. For the butcher and the baker and the candlestick-maker do not dispense *their* wares gratuitously; and Josh Boyles would, perhaps, never dream of asking a thing of them which he asks of the doctor as a matter of course.

Josh Boyles goes away, and an hour or two later, when the doctor and his wife are wrapped in slumber, there comes a knock at the door which brings the wife at one bound to the middle of the room, with her heart palpitating in her throat and a dire fear in her mind that some risen Hercules or some avenging Nemesis has descended upon the little house and its inmates to annihilate them from the face of the earth. The doctor is wide awake, too, and, hastily putting on one or two garments, goes boldly forth to meet the invading foe. He opens the door and finds—a timid maiden standing there. She had run a quarter of a mile through the darkness, and her fear and breathlessness and anxiety for the patient—who was "having a fit" —had nerved her arm to give a knock which will echo through the corridors of time,—at least, the doctor's wife hears it echoing still, and a good many years have gone by since that night. The maiden herself was, perhaps, never conscious of the mighty power she had put into it, unless her knuckles may have given her an inkling of it afterward.

But the doctor dresses and goes forth into the night; the wife drops into a short sleep, from which she is awakened a half-hour later by the doctor's return. The light is soon extinguished, and all is still and sleep comes once more.

It is not long, or it does not seem long, until the wife, who is not sleeping very profoundly, hears footsteps on the walk and then a knock. She awakens her husband, who goes with a sigh toward the door. The next instant the sigh gives place to an exclamation which, if not profane, is something very near it. The wife smothers a laugh, for she knows that *she* is always careful to set the chairs back so that the coast will be clear between the bed and the door; and hence he will have to lay the blame upon himself for setting that chair out when he came in, an hour or two before. He reaches the door, and, not knowing the nature or condition of the caller, curbs his anger as best he may and asks, in a kind of neutral and uncertain voice, " What is it ? " A voice responds, " Why, Doc., I wish you'd come down and see my wife as quick as you can."

The doctor knows now who is there, and his voice is no longer uncertain. His wrath is augmented by the fact that it has been curbed needlessly.

" The devil to it! And what's the matter with her now ? "

" W'y, she's got a pain in her side and she's a-swellin' up."

" *Yes, she's swelling up.*"

This emphatic and quite

unusual acquiescence in his diagnosis of the case seems to puzzle the man in outer darkness. His inner darkness prevents his recognition of so fine and subtle a thing as sarcasm, especially as it proceeds from a hitherto good-natured doctor. So, after an instant of silence, he says, "Yes— she—seems to be swellin' a right smart."

The doctor, who has a pretty clear idea as to how much she is likely to be "swellin'," tells the man to go home and put a mustard draft upon her, and that he will be down early in the morning; then closes the door and gropes his way to bed, saying, as he comes, "Poor devils that haven't got anything, that don't know anything, and that you can't teach anything are the kind that come to wake a fellow up from his sleep."

"Yes," says his wife, "this is the third charity call to-night; but, all the same, I know you were glad, for once in your life, that this was a charity call."

"How do you happen to know that?"

"I happen to know that a man has a longing

to express himself when he has just stubbed his toes unmercifully."

The doctor laughs, but makes no denial, and in a few minutes is snoring away as peacefully as though his sleep had not been interrupted. Not so the wife. She cannot get to sleep this time, and, if she could, is afraid some one will come and arouse her again, in which case she will not sleep for the rest of the night. So she lies awake and thinks her own thoughts while silence "broods like a gentle spirit o'er the still and pulseless world." It is past midnight, and the cocks have been proclaiming the "holy hour."

The doctor sleeps on.

His wife lies awake for a long time, then she hears quick footsteps. Are they coming this way or going the other way? She listens. They are coming this way. Will they go by or will they stop? They stop. Then begins a series of nudgings and callings. The nudging and the calling are both very moderate at first, but, producing not the slightest impression on the sleeping doctor, they wax more and more vigorous till, by

THE PHYSICIAN'S WIFE.

the time the knock has sounded, he is brought to a sitting posture and a very, very sleepy "Yes" responds to the knock.

This time it is one of his prompt-paying patrons, for whom it is a pleasure to practice. He wants the doctor to come to his house just as quick as he can get there, and is quite breathless in his haste.

"All right; I'll be down right away."

The door is closed and the caller goes with hurried footsteps down the walk. Then the doctor calmly and deliberately—*so* deliberately—proceeds to get himself ready; to dress himself with most scrupulous care, as it seems to his impatient wife, whose sympathies are always with the patient. By and by he is far enough along to sit down and draw his boots to his side. He takes one by either strap and—falls into a reverie! There he sits, a motionless figure; his head bent slightly forward and his eyes in a wide stare. The poor man has been losing sleep every night for a week, perhaps; but his wife can only think of that breathless man and his message. She endures as long as she can; then she fidgets with as much noise as she can possibly make, and gives vent to a mighty sigh.

He heeds it not.

She passes another minute in silent agony; then exclaims, with purposely explosive force, "*Doctor!* Are you asleep?"

He comes to himself at that; and finally the boots are on, and he rises and starts in the direction of his collar. His wife meekly suggests that he might just button his coat up close, and go without his collar and cravat,—no one would know the difference; and, since he can button his coat clear up to his ears and down to his waist, it would not make a bit of difference if he should go without his shirt! *Anything* when that man was in such a hurry for him to come. But he doesn't do it; he never does. He has lived long enough to know that the danger in those cases is very seldom so imminent as the friends of the patient think, and that it is much more sensible not to go at a high-pressure speed too often. It would rob him of that very coolness and calmness which make a physician's presence in the sick-room so comforting and so re-assuring.

But his wife is immensely relieved when the door closes behind him and she hears his quick tread on the walk. No laggard movement now. It is not long until he is back and in bed once more, and this time sleep condescends to visit both the doctor and his wife. They sleep very soundly, but after awhile are aroused by a "Hello!" from the gate, which, from the emphasis placed upon it, has probably been repeated several times before in a milder tone. The doctor goes to the door, and opens it. It is early dawn now, and he can see a hale young fellow from the country sitting on his horse.

"What's wanted, young man?"

"John Smith came over a little bit ago to get me to come after you. He wants you to come out to his house right away."

"All right. What's the matter out there now?"

"I don't know; bees aswarmin', I guess."

And off he rides, leaving the doctor to interpret this mystic message as best he may.

And so he is gone again, and the night is past.

Perhaps the next night the doctor and his wife will both enjoy a night of unbroken rest. Let us hope so. But when another night has come he must be away again. He tells his wife he may not be back till morning, and, as she has been a little timid about staying alone since the neighbor's house was robbed, she gets a young lady across the street to come in and stay with her, and, to still better fortify themselves, they sleep together.

About 2 o'clock they are aroused by a big knock that the doctor's wife recognizes, and she says, in a hurried undertone, "Oh, it's the doctor!" Then there is "mounting in hot haste," and the wild fluttering of a night-gown disappearing into an adjoining room, while the doctor is admitted at the front door.

When 9 o'clock comes, the next night, the wife finds herself feeling a little restless and uneasy. She has just been reading a powerful story, in a leading magazine, in which a murder has been committed. She wishes her husband would come, and hopes most fervently that he will be at home with her to-night. Pretty soon she hears his footsteps,—and he *will* be home to-night! He comes in more hastily than usual, and asks for his overcoat, as he is going to the country and may need it before he gets back.

"Oh, dear; do you have to go again to-night?"

"Yes; I have to go."

"Will you be gone all night?"

"Oh, no; I'll be back in a few hours;" adding, with a smile, "so it won't be worth while to get Lucy to come and stay with you, will it?"

"No; not at all. Besides, she is asleep by this time, I dare say."

He goes out into the night again, and she goes to the door and casts a wistful eye over to the house where Lucy lives. It is shrouded in darkness; and she does wish they would not retire so early over there. The thought comes into her mind that perhaps Lucy has retired early in self-defense; then she carefully bolts every door and fastens every window, and, after that is done, she seats herself in her big chair again. She pushes the magazine aside,—she is a little afraid of it,—and picks up a favorite volume of poems, always lying where she can put her hand on it. She reads for awhile, and by and by the old charm begins to assert itself, and she loses in some degree her sensations of fear and loneliness. After awhile she closes the little volume, and prepares to retire. The first thing she does in her preparations is to go to her closet, take out a linen duster that hangs there, and lay it on the back of a chair at the foot of the bed. Then she goes out through the hall, unlocks the door leading on to the back porch, stoops down and picks up the little puppy asleep in his box, hurries through the door as if the Furies were behind her, bolts it, carries the little black pup—whining a little at being disturbed—into her sleeping-room, and lays him gently down in the chimney-corner. She does not make preparations of this kind when the doctor is at home; but it is really company for her to have some living, breathing thing in the room besides herself. She puts the duster by the bed, so it will be handy in case burglars should come. When they come, she is going to jump into it and run to the next neighbor's. She turns the light down very low, and goes to bed.

After awhile the clock chimes out the hour of eleven. It is high time for her to be asleep, but she is not asleep. A half-hour goes by. How still it is! The clock's dull tick and an occasional little snore from the puppy are the only sounds she hears.

The clock ticks on. Midnight is drawing near,—the strange and solemn time which lies between the day that is dead and the day that is just born. Another day, with all its possibilities for good, will in another moment take its place in the eternal past, and the opportunities that might have been hers, if she had only been alert and ready to "grasp the skirts of happy chance," are gone, and gone forever.

The clock is striking. The day is dead. And as another from out the great ranks of the future steps into the narrow niche where yesterday has stood and becomes to-day, she wonders if it will be any different with her in this new day. How will it be through all the days that are to come? If she live to be an old, white-haired woman, will she feel then, as she does to-night, that her life has been slothful and inactive, and that, for any good thing that she has accomplished in her little world, she might as well have never lived at all?

Her eyes wander to the dear little volume on the table, and her thoughts stray westward to the grave on the mountain-side where its gifted author lies at rest, "clover-blossoms on her breast."

Her life and her work were grand and beautiful and live after her yet. In that little book, in exquisitely pathetic lines, is the record of her deep humility and grief, when the end of life drew near, that she had done no more. It is her last prayer, and so she has named it:—

"Father, I scarcely dare to pray,
　So clear I see, now it is done,
That I have wasted half my day,
　And left my work but just begun;
*　*　*　*　*　*　*
"So clear I see that I have hurt
　The souls I might have helped to save;
That I have slothful been, inert,
　Deaf to the calls thy leaders gave.

"In outskirts of thy kingdoms vast,
　Father, the humblest spot give me;
Set me the lowliest task thou hast;
　Let me repentant work for thee!"

This woman, with all her glorious work for a misunderstood and down-trodden race behind her, as well as her work for the most cultured of her time, cannot find it in her heart at last to ask a place within the courts of heaven, but only asks the humblest spot in the *outskirts* of the kingdom, where she may be given the meanest and lowliest work to do, and she will do it willingly, repentantly, for the Master, because of what she has left undone on earth.

There are tears in the eyes of the doctor's wife as she thinks of this life, too soon ended, and of the deep, deep humility that is breathed forth in this "Last Prayer." When the last hour shall come to her, and to others like her who have done so little, what will there be left for them to ask?

Then her thoughts wander off to the cultured woman who has taken up the work her gifted predecessor let fall, and it is some pleasure to her to reflect that she is a physician's wife. But her thoughts are interrupted by most welcome footsteps, and now the doctor's wife grows both brave and sleepy; for the doctor has come, and she is safe, and knows nothing more till morning.

And so the nights come and go,—some of them spent in unbroken sleep, some of them cut into fragments. The wife learns to accept the broken nights philosophically and gracefully. It is all a part of her life. And what of the doctor, himself, as he goes on his midnight journeys? Happy is he, since he must be abroad so often in the night, if he can draw himself away for awhile from sickness and want and all temporal things, and find some beauty or grandeur in a silent world or in the skies of midnight. Does he ever pause for an instant, in his lonely walks, to look up into the starry vault that bends above him? Perhaps; and if so, it may be that he is able to read there a message for him,— weary worker while all the world lies sleeping,— some sweet and comforting message  "writ in the jewelled cypher of the night." Or it may be that, driving, some stormy night, through swaying trees and blinding rain, with the fitful flashing of the lightning for his guide, and the crash and roar of the thunder all about him, he can "look through Nature up to Nature's God," and feel a closer kinship with the mighty hand that rules the elements at war than with the hand that rules when all is peace. For there comes a turbulence into the souls of men sometimes which revels in the storm, and perhaps that turbulence has not been entirely eliminated from the soul of the doctor.

The physician's **wife** should possess some tact and discretion, and her bump of curiosity should be not too largely developed. When the doctor comes home, it is more than probable he will enjoy talking about something else than what has occupied his mind at the office. Then she should not greet him with a round of questions and cross-questions as to this or that patient, just what is the matter with him or her, etc., etc. In the first place, there are many things she has no right to know. Patients are often very sensitive; they take the doctor into their confidence because they must, not because they would choose to do so if it could be avoided. That confidence should not be betrayed even to his wife. In the next place, she should not want to know. It will often be a relief to her to say, if she is questioned,—and to say honestly and without evasion,—I do not know. By this I do not mean that the physician should never mention his patients to his wife; but it might not be amiss for him, in some cases, to carry in his memory the words of Hotspur to Lady Percy, his wife, when she begged him to reveal to her an important secret:—

"Thou wilt not utter what thou dost not know;
And so far will I trust thee, gentle Kate."

Then he kindly goes on,—

"I know you wise, but yet no farther wise
Than Harry Percy's wife; constant you are,
But yet a woman; and, for secrecy,
No lady closer."

That was nearly five hundred years ago, and Harry Percy no doubt voiced the sentiment of his time. Let us hope, however, that the physician will not find it necessary to refuse his wife his confidence because, like Hotspur, he is afraid to trust her, but simply because he has no right to reveal these things, and she has no right to know them. And let us hope that all physicians, as well as all other men, recognize now that if Hotspur could come back and look with observant eyes on the world he left so long ago, he would see with very clear vision that, while secrets still continue to escape their moorings, his indiscreet brethren have as large a share in their release as his indiscreet sisters, and that the equality of men and women is being more and more established on the earth.

Physicians' wives are denied some privileges which other wives may enjoy if they care to do so. For instance, if anybody needs a big, savage dog, it is certainly the doctor's wife, who is so often left without a protector in the night. Yet she is the very one who cannot have a savage dog, because he would bite the people who come for the doctor at night just as quick as he would a burglar or a tramp, which would not be profitable for any of the parties concerned.

Most physicians do not relish the idea of their wives sleeping over loaded revolvers either; since they, coming in at all hours of the night and arousing said wives suddenly, might, in a frenzied moment or in some interrupted dream, be mistaken for midnight marauders and be fired upon accordingly.

Then, if the doctor's wife go to church or to the opera-house with her husband she is liable to have to go home through the darkness alone, somebody else having a more urgent claim on the doctor than she. However, while I do not feel called upon to give my reason for the statement, I will say that I believe very few doctors have to leave church to answer calls.

Then, too, it has long been considered a prerogative of wives to indulge in little hysterical fits occasionally, as a means to compass an end. It is said to be a very effectual means, and that nothing scares and subdues the average man like hysterics. The physician's wife is forever debarred from this high privilege,—that is, if she have the discernment to see which way her best interests lie. Her husband would neither be frightened, subdued, nor sympathetic. He "knows the symptoms."

I have sometimes wondered about this queer disease, and have said to the doctor of our household, "Hysteria *is* a real disease, is it not?" He admits rather reluctantly that it is. Still, he does not admit that it deserves any sympathy whatever, but that, on the contrary, only the most "heroic" treatment; and I am pretty sure all doctors hold the same view. Now, I find, in reading the history of the disease, that it is a disordered condition of the nervous system; that hereditary predisposition to nerve-instability is its most prolific cause, though the want of occupation is also a prolific cause; that the depressing effects of almost any disease may produce it, especially if the disease be accompanied by much pain and loss of sleep; that in hysteria one of the commonest sensations is that of a nail being driven through the top of the head; that the senses of taste, sight, and hearing may be affected,—sometimes temporarily obliterated; that it may pass into absolute insanity. All this on the authority of a man eminent in the medical profession.

I am making no plea for "hysterics." Even if I were not a physician's wife, I should hope never to "have 'em" myself; but I will say that it seems to me one may find some excuse for the poor creatures who are victims to all or to any of the sensations just mentioned; and I defy any disdainful doctor to experience just one of the above-named sensations,—viz., to feel that some monster stands, Jael-like, with hammer and nail to pierce the vertex of *his* skull,—and not "take on."

Then, since the want of occupation is one of the chief causes of hysteria, that should teach him charity, lest he, too, should one day become hysterical. And he need not feel that he enjoys absolute immunity from this tabooed disease himself, for there is another statement in that same able article,—to the effect that for every twenty hysterical women there is one hysterical man! I was overjoyed to find it. I had always supposed, as far as any written or printed record of the matter was concerned, that our sex enjoyed an odious monopoly of hysterics; and one out of twenty in such a matter is no small percentage. But, right here comes in another statement,—that a chief characteristic of the disease is a desire to be an object of importance; and that seems to me to make the percentage much too small. I really cannot harmonize that statement with the one that there is only one hysterical man to twenty hysterical women.

The article tells me, too, that another characteristic is a constant craving for sympathy. It may be one would have to go very far back in the history of the race to get at the root of that matter. Here, it seems to me, the percentage should be equal, for, whether or not we ever admit it to ourselves or to others, we all know, men and women alike, that deep down in the heart there is a longing for some appreciation, some love, some sympathy. And, if the love and sympathy had always existed that should exist between man and his brother-man, between woman and her sister-woman, and between men and women, who need not stand in opposing ranks, but as friends and counselors each to the other, since both have like hopes and ambitions, and both must walk alike the pleasant and the weary paths of life, then there would be no motive for even an occasional exhibition to the doctor of a morbid and offensive craving for sympathy which, naturally enough, can only awaken contempt in his professional mind.

But things are as they are, and not as they should be, and we must accept them until a better order shall come to reign.

ALL men are absent-minded and forgetful; but I believe physicians are particularly so, thereby causing a world of inconvenience to their wives. In this I have found much unanimity of opinion among physicians' wives of my acquaintance, though justice usually leads them to admit that the doctor has a better excuse for his absent-mindedness than most men. His mind as he goes from breakfast may be ever so firmly fixed on what he is to order for dinner, or upon any other commission he meant to execute for his wife, but for him exigencies are always arising. It may be a broken bone, or a man bleeding to death, or a baby choking to death; and it is really no wonder that the poor man's plans and purposes "gang aft aglee." In cases of this kind all charity should be extended to the doctor, even though his wife be compelled, for a day or two at a time, to take no thought as to what she shall eat or wherewith she shall be clothed; but she should not condone too lightly *all* the sins of a treacherous memory by which she is so often placed in very trying positions.

One pretty young doctor's wife was telling me, not long ago, a little experience of hers which she assured me was only one of many.

One winter morning, just after her husband had gone from breakfast, the busy wife was startled by a knock at the kitchen-door, near which she was standing. She opened it, and there stood Auntie J., a voluble but kind-hearted woman, well known in the neighborhood. She carried a basket on her arm, and she walked in and seated herself, set the basket down beside her, took off her hood and laid it on the basket, and began warming her feet. The doctor's wife was naturally somewhat surprised at the earliness of her call, and at the comfortable way in which her visitor settled herself, as if for the day; but she inquired as to the welfare of her family, as people always do, and they chatted away for awhile, though the methodical little wife, casting an uneasy eye around her small domain, could not help wishing that Auntie had waited till she got the breakfast-dishes washed and the house put in order for the day. By and by Auntie quietly inquired,

" Well, are you about ready for me to begin ?"

" Begin *what?*"

" Well, for the land's sake! Hain't Doc. told you nothin' about it ?"

" The doctor has told me nothing about *anything,*" said the little woman, in indignant,

yet despairing tones. "What is it you are to begin?"

"Why, he told me last night to come down this morning and help you with the butcherin'."

Deep silence on the part of the doctor's wife, who felt herself too full for utterance.

"He said there'd be some men down here to do the out-door work, and for me to come to help *you*."

Now, "butchering" was something the soul of the doctor's wife did not delight in. She knew something about it *in toto*, but very little as to detail, and, while it was the custom at that time for families in the town to superintend the preparing and putting away of the supply of meats for the year, yet this young wife felt, to the depths of her soul, as she walked to the window and gazed out with blurred vision upon the wintry landscape, that it was a custom more honored in the breach than in the observance. And then to think that the doctor had not told her anything at all about it—simply forgot it —and just sent a lot of people down there and left her no way to help herself. Oh! she wishes she had never got married, or, at any rate, that she had not married a man whose wits went so often wool-gathering, and then she would not have to be standing there now with a lump in her throat that would not down, and kept threatening every minute to choke her. She can hear those heartless men now, whistling and singing as if their work were the greatest joy of their lives, and as if a heart inside the house were not ready to burst with its impotent wrath and scorn of it all!

Auntie takes in the situation, but bustles around outwardly oblivious. The doctor's wife gets through her work and the morning somehow. Auntie is there to dinner, but the doctor is not. Is he away in the country, or have his wandering senses come back to tell him of the probable state of affairs at home, and to remind him that it might be expedient for him to dine at a restaurant to-day? That is one great advantage the doctor has; he is away so often necessarily that he can stay sometimes unnecessarily, and yet have no comment excited by his absence. (I hope doctors do not often take so mean an advantage of confiding and trustful wives.)

After dinner comes the tug of war, and the young wife stands like a stoic at a table, with a big colored man on one side of her, and  a white man, whom she strongly suspects to be a thief, on the other side, with Auntie at the end, and together they cut and cross-cut and slash the huge pieces of fat preparatory to "rendering" out the lard, while the lean meat is put into a big tub to be ground into sausage. When at last that part of it is done, and the men are out about the kettles again, Auntie and the doctor's wife seat themselves on two chairs opposite each other, Auntie to "feed" and the doctor's wife to "grind."

And she grinds and she grinds, and her thoughts go off to the mills of the gods, which are said to grind slowly and exceeding small; and she thinks that this mill, which her unanimated muscles are manipulating, is a good deal like those mills of the gods. Presently, Auntie says, "I'll rest ye a bit"; and when the two have changed places the grinding goes on and on. After a long silence Auntie remarks, as she turns steadily away at the crank, "I hee'rd a preacher preach oncet about two wimmen a-grindin' at a mill."

A smile—which the doctor's wife would repress if she could, for she does not want Auntie to think that she could be weak enough to so far forget her trials as to smile this day—plays about her mouth, as she replies, "It wasn't a sausage-mill, was it, Auntie?"

"I reckon it must 'a been. I don't b'leeve I ever seen two wimmin a-grindin' away at any other kind of a mill. The preacher said one of them would be took and the other left. I don't jist know what he meant by that." Here Auntie looked up at her companion and a merry gleam came into her eyes, as she added, "But its my opinion that if anybody is a-comin' for one of us, they'll have a hard time a-choosin' which one to take and which one to leave."

The doctor's wife, looking at the frowzy head of her companion, which looks just like her own head feels, and at the greased hands and aprons of the twain, feels very sure that in this case both grinding women would be left.

But all things come to an end, and so at last does the grinding. The doctor's wife remarks, wearily, that she does not know what she is expected to do with that immense tub of sausage, because the doctor does not like sausage much, and she doesn't either. Auntie, who is a thrifty and business-like soul, looks at her in a kind of pitying disdain.

"Well, good land, child, why didn't ye sell yer pigs, then? What did ye butcher fer?"

"What did *I* butcher for!"

The doctor's wife looks at Auntie with blazing eyes and withering scorn. The last straw has broken the camel's back. Auntie is answered.

Later in the evening she carried home with her a generous portion of the contents of the tub. The colored man also came in for a goodly share, and the white man of questionable integrity was given a somewhat smaller portion, as seemed to the hostess fitting and proper.

That night the doctor's wife—and the doctor —had an interesting conference together on the subject of absent-mindedness, and, when that was through, on the subject of butchering, and they mutually and severally agreed that the lord-high-executioner of the town's pigs should be employed at his own headquarters on all future occasions, provided there was ever any more butchering to do.

Another doctor's wife relates a little incident, in regard to her husband's absent-mindedness, which was really quite surprising to me, well accustomed as I am to surprising things.

It seems they had two ministers at their house to dinner one day,—both of them D.D.s, I think she said,—when her good husband, instead of asking one of them to pronounce the blessing, started to pronounce it himself. If he could have gone entirely through with it without recollecting himself, all would have been well; but in the midst of it his senses returned; he halted, stammered; his wife grew hot and cold by turns; but at last it was finished up in some way, and the meal begun amid some slightly affected coughing and some remarks not specially pertinent.

Now, it did seem to me a most astonishing thing that *a doctor* should start in ahead of two ministers to ask a blessing, be he ever so absent-minded; but when I found that he was in the *habit* of saying grace at his own table, my amazement was complete. I was very glad, indeed, to hear of him. He lives in Indiana. I have also heard of one more. He lives in New York. Isolated cases are always interesting to the profession, and the profession, too, will be glad to know of them. It will also be glad to know that, however doubtful these two States may be politically, yet morally they are forging to the front!

Then I go back in my own memory to an autumn evening eleven years ago, and see myself standing just outside the gate, in earnest conversation with a man in a wagon. He had driven up with the announcement that "Doc. told me to bring these chickens down to you; there's jist a dozen of 'em." That was in the first year of our married life, and we were living in a new little house, rented, on a new little place with not a shed nor a coop where chickens might be even temporarily stowed; and where *could* I put the chickens? In my anxiety and bewilderment, is it any wonder that my thoughts turned finally and very reluctantly to one stiff little room in our house we never used except when "callers" came? That night, when the doctor came home and found the chickens safe and apparently sound, he confided to me the fact that after ordering the man to bring them down he had started out in town to visit a patient, when all at once the thought struck him that I had not an earthly place to put them when they got there. Of course he knew that before, but he was absent-minded. He turned around intending to come home and see about it, and then went on his way again, saying to himself, "I'll warrant she'll manage them!" And not a wave of trouble rolled across his peaceful breast. My sisters, that was a sublime faith, and those were halcyon days, when the faith, and especially the expression of it, were balm and incense to my soul. But St. Paul has something very pointed to say about faith without works, and if the same thing should occur to-morrow I should say, "A little less faith, Doctor dear, and a chicken-coop."

I will add that, while my thoughts did fly to the parlor, I did not put the chickens there. An inspiration came just in time, and I asked the man to leave his coop until he came to town again, and in the meantime I would have one made.

If I were to stop to chronicle all the instances that might be chronicled of the absent-mindedness of physicians, this little volume would stretch out into a very unwieldy one, which I have pledged myself shall not happen. So I leave this fruitful and inviting theme behind me.

AND now I would like to ask physicians' wives, Do your husbands ever get sick? Then, angels and ministers of grace defend you! A doctor is so accustomed to being director in a sick-room that he wants to be director at the same time that he is the patient, when he is not at himself and not capable of directing things. I have been so fortunate as to have had only one experience in that line, but it clings to my memory still. It is not anarchy nor rebellion of any kind that I am advocating when I advise you, as one who knows whereof she speaks, to keep a high hand and not let the patient gain the ascendancy over you, or reason and common sense will flee away and folly run riot in your household.

One physician's wife of my acquaintance tells me that her husband nearly drove her wild during an illness of his. She says that, while he was too sick to have the management of himself and his room entirely in his own hands as he wanted to have, he was still not sick enough to care nothing about those things and yield himself to others; and a patient of that kind, even when he is not a doctor, is very hard to manage.

It was in the month of November when he was taken ill, and many of the days were bleak and cold; yet he would insist on the door and every window in the room being open, while blinds banged and curtains flapped, and the free winds of heaven had frolicsome times in his apartment.

His wife told me that she remembered one cold, raw morning in particular, when, fearful that he would take cold, she begged him to consent to have one window and the outside door closed, which would still leave two windows open; but when he fiercely charged her with cruelty, a fell purpose to smother him, etc., she desisted. Soon afterward a physician from a neighboring village, who happened to be in town, came down to call upon his sick brother.

The wife conducted him to the sick-room, saw him enter, then glance around with a shiver at the open door and windows and the wildly-flapping curtains, and the next instant she knew that her sick husband had seen the glance and the shiver, too, for she heard a voice from the bed, so meek that it might have proceeded from Moses himself, saying, "Doctor, won't you please close that door and one or two of the windows; I think they have got it too cold in here for me!"

That was more than flesh and blood could stand, and the doctor's wife walked majestically into that room and explained to the new-comer exactly why "they" had it too cold in there for the sick man.

She gives another instance of the sick doctor's way of doing things. One evening, after she had given her husband a bath and made all comfortable for the night, her brother, who had just arrived from another State on a short visit, insisted that she retire for a good night's rest, while he would lie down near the patient and attend to anything necessary through the night. There would be very little to attend to, as the doctor had little or no fever, and was not to be awakened for anything whatever if he slept. The wife knew that when bed-time came reproaches would be heaped upon her for leaving him, but she also knew her own frame, and duty and common sense told her that if she would be well and strong for the morrow she must sleep, especially since her husband was in good condition, and her brother was an excellent nurse in case any nursing were required, and the patient would probably go to sleep and sleep all night.

Accordingly, at 9 o'clock, steeling herself against the reproachful looks and glances, which came sure enough, she bade her husband good-night and retired to rest.

About 2 o'clock she was awakened by a noise, and opening her eyes beheld a tall, barefooted figure, with one suspender over its shoulder and one at its side, wandering helplessly about with a tea-kettle in its hand. The doctor's wife rose instantly to a sitting posture and demanded, "Jack, what in this world are you trying to do?"

"Why, the doctor called me just now, and said he wanted to take a bath."

"Take a bath! He just took one at bed-time."

"Well, that is what he said, and I was trying to find things without waking you, but I couldn't find anything but this tea-kettle."

Of course he couldn't. Where is the man that could find things, even if he were master of the house and knew just where they were, until his wife went and calmly and instantly placed them in his hands.

"Never mind, Jack. I'll get dressed and attend to it; and you lie down here, where you can sleep."

She dressed herself, and went out into the

kitchen to get kindling to replenish the fire, which had burned too low to heat water. Finding no kindling there, she groped her way out into the wood-shed, where she was more fortunate. When the fire was rebuilt and the water heated, she went in to tell her patient that all was ready. He looked calmly up into her face, and announced that he had just concluded to wait till morning!

But he did'nt. He took his bath right then. And afterward, as morning was so near, the good wife just sat down beside the patient, who became as happy and contented as a little child when its mother is near. She knew, as well as if he had told her, that his reason for wanting a bath at that time was only an excuse to get her there with him, and, unreasonable as it might be, now that it was all over it did not displease her. She only looked down upon the good face now sinking into contented sleep, and the thought of the utter reliance of the strong man, in his weakness, upon one frail woman touched her very deeply. She bent down and gently pressed her cheek to the hand that, even in sleep, still clasped her own, and made up her mind that to-morrow night, come what would, she would stay by or near him the whole night. But when the doctor was well again they had some merry laughs over it all, and he was able to realize then, as fully as his wife had done in his illness, that he was a most unsaintly patient.

I have heard of just one man who was as unreasonable as a sick doctor can be, and he was an old sailor who, having spent all his life upon the sea, concluded, in the evening of his days, to marry and settle down on shore. But he missed the sound of the dashing and rolling waves so much that he never could get to sleep at night until his wife went out and dashed buckets of water up on the window-panes till he was soothed off to slumber. I have often thought of that faithful wife as she toiled away at her nightly task, and have wondered what were the wild waves saying to *her*.

This same doctor's wife fell

quite ill a month or two after her husband's recovery, and it was remarked throughout the house how very much easier it was to care for her than it had been to care for the doctor. She was convalescent,—indeed, almost well again,—when it became necessary for her husband to leave home for a day or two on business. He came down the evening before he was to start, made his preliminary preparations, and the family retired early, in order to get the doctor off on an early train in the morning. The doctor soon grew sleepy. Not so his wife. She was meditating. Just as the first faint snore rose from the other side of the bed, a quiet but distinct voice said, "Doctor, won't you please get up and heat some water? I believe I ought to have a warm bath."

The doctor was awake on the instant.

"Gee—whiz! *To-night?*"

"Yes; I think it would be best to have it to-night, if it *is* cold, while you are here to help me."

A moment of silence; then a terrific sigh

rent the darkness, as the doctor slowly raised himself on one elbow. Another mighty sigh, and he succeeded in gaining a sitting posture.

"I am sorry I didn't think of it sooner, dear, but I suppose it is better late than never."

What the doctor supposed on that point he hardly liked to say to an invalid, and that invalid his wife, for fear she might think he did not want to take the trouble to do things for her, while, of course, it was not that at all. Besides, his own experience as an invalid was pretty fresh in his mind, and so there seemed absolutely nothing for this doctor to do but to do as his wife had so gently requested. So the covers were pushed back, and slowly his feet sought the floor. He got entirely up at last, took a few steps, drew his breath sharply, and remarked that it was enough to give a man the lock-jaw to step on that oil-cloth. He proceeded, with many a grunt and groan,—not wholly involuntary,—toward the kitchen.

A voice, as steady as circumstances would permit, came from the bed: "I am awfully sorry to trouble you so much, but you will find the tub out in the wood-shed, on the other side of that pile of stove-wood."

The good wife thought she saw the atmosphere around the doctor take on the hue of sulphuric flame, but she was an invalid; so all she heard was, "Good God! I hope you don't have to have a tub!"

Then a merry peal of laughter rang out on the doctor's delighted ear. He understood, now, that he had only been asked to swallow a small spoonful of his own medicine, and came back to bed a happier and a wiser man.

It would be much better for the doctor's wife never to get sick, if she could so arrange matters. She is placed at a disadvantage, in many ways, by getting sick. I call to mind an instance: This physician was a very absent-minded man in his waking hours, but in his sleep there was nothing to compare with him. At one time his wife was ill,—hardly enough so to require night-watchers, but too ill to get up and do things for herself. One night she grew very thirsty, and concluded to arouse the doctor, if she could, and have him bring her a glass of fresh water from the pump. After exhausting all ordinary means to awaken him, she took the glass of water sitting near, which had become too warm to drink, and poured a little of it down the doctor's back. This brought him up in bed, with a dazed look on his face.

"*Doctor!* Wake up! Listen! Go out to the pump,—*pump*, do you hear? the *pump!*—and bring me a glass of water."

The doctor got slowly out of bed, and, to his wife's delight, took the glass she offered him and went straight to the pump. He left the door ajar, and from her place in bed his wife saw him set the glass down under the spout, as he would have done a bucket, and begin pumping. When the glass was filled he did not stop. When the floor of the porch where the pump stood was deluged he did not stop. When five minutes had gone by, the doctor was still pumping. His wife, who had been alternately shrieking at him and moaning to herself during those long, slow minutes, now lay quiet and resigned. She realized that she had fixed the idea of pumping thoroughly into his beclouded mind, and that there was nothing for her to do but lie there and listen to the deluge, and let him pump on. He pumped for about two minutes longer, and then came in without the glass of water! The poor, thirst-consumed wife had to see him get back into bed and to realize that he had not been awake at all, and she thinks she learned that night "how sublime a thing it is to suffer and be strong."

Illness on the part of a doctor's wife places her at a disadvantage in another way. Any other woman in the world has the privilege, or ought to have the privilege, of choosing her own physician; but she must choose her husband for her physician, whether she wants him or not. It would be a very delicate matter for her to tell him, though she do it ever so gently, that she would rather have some other doctor when she is sick. She would feel like the colored minister who was asked by a gentleman to preach a sermon to his flock on the sin of chicken-stealing. This the colored brother was unwilling to do, giving as his reason that it would be " ap' to frow a col'ness ober de meetin'."

The doctor would be very likely to look at the matter from the stand-point of what people would think and say about it. Such action on his wife's part would seem to him an open confession that she had more confidence in some other physician than in her own husband, and that might lead other folks to the conclusion that *they* had more confidence in some other physician, too, which would not only be very humiliating to the doctor, but would place his very bread and butter in jeopardy. Thus he would overlook entirely the real motive which would actuate her in her choice. It would not be that she had no confidence in the high character, both moral and professional, of her husband, but that she, in common with her sex and with the whole race, had something of the innate tendency to choose the physician least known to the patient personally; to choose the unknown and untried in preference to the tried and true. How often does the unknown, with the mystery that attaches to him, exercise a charm over us which the possibly greater merits of the known have never done! A great many people never stop to reflect, indeed have never learned, that

> "The distant pyramids of stone
> That wedge-like cleave the desert airs,
> When nearer seen and better known,
> Are but gigantic flights of stairs."

They do not care to get near enough to the pyramids to learn the secret of their construction. They like mystery. They like to stand afar off in awed wonderment, and view them from that distance which lends enchantment.

So, if there should ever be a physician's wife courageous enough—or foolish enough, whichever you please—to confess to her husband that she wants some other doctor to attend her when she is sick (and as yet I have never heard of her), I trust that he will look at the matter exactly as he would if any other of his patients expressed a preference for somebody else; since there is nothing in her composition to render her entirely different from the rest of the race; and then he can go on his way philosophically and undismayed, as he does in other cases of the kind.

Then it is a disadvantage for the physician's wife to be sick, or to have her husband get sick, for another reason. I have heard people express great and apparently sincere surprise that I, a doctor's wife, should ever get sick. And in the case of the doctor himself, surprise has given place to open-eyed amazement. I have sometimes admitted in reply that a doctor ought not to get sick, of course; that he had no business to do so; but that, unfortunately, he was constructed about like other people, with the same physical frame and the same liability to sickness, disease, or accident, with the liability increased in his case by the exposures to which he is subjected. While other people may sweetly dream the night away in their warm beds, he may be driving along through storm and midnight darkness toward some broken bridge, or perilously near some deep ravine, or he may be standing in some hovel where contagious disease holds sway. No; the wonder is not that physicians are ever sick, but that they are not sick much oftener than they are.

When the doctor is sick he is capable, as we have seen, of growing despotic. Perhaps one reason for this may be that it is only a step from autocrat to despot; and when he is well he makes an excellent autocrat, as many physicians' wives have occasion to know. He is so accustomed to having his way and his say in the sick-room, which is right, that he wants to be the autocrat of the breakfast-table, the dinner-table, the tea-table, and the time between tables,—which is *not* right.

One physician's wife cheerfully testifies (one may as well be cheerful in these matters, even though the cheerfulness lies in the testifying, and not in the thing testified of) that for years she has gone without things she likes to eat, because the other side of the house decides they are not good for her. Now, if she were the wife of a lawyer or a merchant, or of any man but a physician, of course she would and should rebel. But a physician is supposed to speak as one having authority in these things, and she maintains a becoming silence. Sometimes, it is true, she has had her little misgivings that the reason certain things are not good for her is that the doctor himself does not like them; for, in the occasional absences of her good husband from home, has not her table speedily reveled in these same forbidden fruits, and have they ever done her any harm? Some day she means to confront him and put him to rout with one of his own sensible utterances made long ago, and doubtless forgotten by him; but wives often have inconveniently good memories, and in cases of this kind, where liberty and the pursuit of happiness are at stake, they should be brought into requisition.

Once upon a time a good while ago this doctor was called in to see an elderly lady who did not have much the matter with her. It was a sort of pleasant pastime on her part to call the young doctor in, since she was a preacher's wife and knew there would be no bill presented. She said, when the doctor went in, "Doctor, I want you to tell me what I ought to eat; this, that, and the other do not seem to agree with me very well."

"How old are you?" was the doctor's blunt inquiry.

Somewhat surprised, she replied that she was a little past fifty.

"Well, if you have lived to be more than fifty years old and have not learned for yourself what you can eat and what you can't eat, its of no use to call me in. You ought to know better than I can tell you." And away went the doctor.

His wife feels that she, too, ought to know

what she can eat, and so it is not improbable that a new *régime* will be established in her household. Of course the drowning doctor will catch at a straw like other drowning men, and will remind her that she has not lived to be past fifty yet; but the flood of her steady and righteous persistence will sweep this straw away, and right and common sense will yet triumph, as they did in another instance where this autocratic doctor lately held brief sway.

He had had a quantity of dirt hauled into his front yard in order to do some much-needed filling up, and had it spread evenly over the surface. It was not long till several dozen cabbage-plants made their appearance in the new soil; some wind-blown seeds had doubtless found lodgment there before it had been brought to the doctor's yard.

The doctor, probably acting upon the assumption that whatever is is right, said, "Now we will just leave these here and have some early cabbage."

His wife, having in mind the eternal fitness of

things, said, "No; when they get a little larger we will transplant them to the garden and have just as early cabbage as if they were left here." She spoke in a quiet, matter-of-fact way, not dreaming of opposition to so sensible a proposition. To her amazement the good doctor declared very emphatically that they should stay right there, and he himself was going to cultivate them

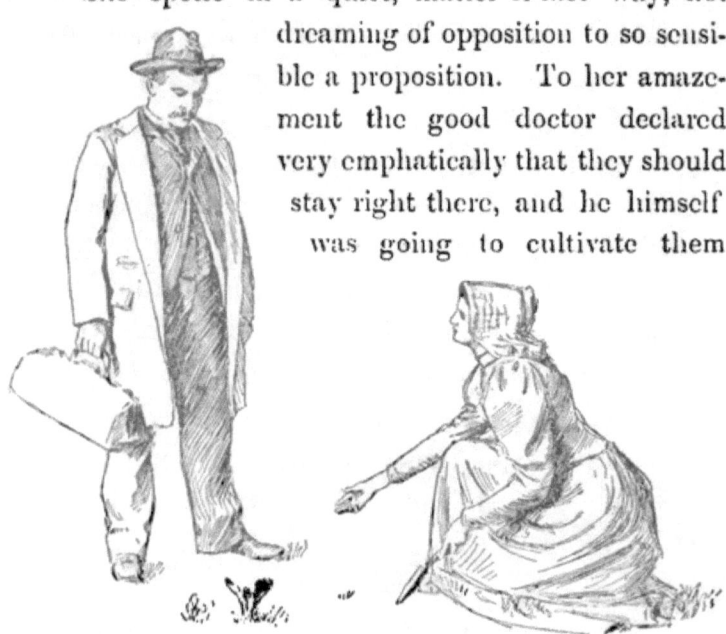

there. Then the wife inquired in earnest tones if he thought she was going to have several dozen great, flaunting, ugly cabbages growing in her front yard; and she also inquired what he supposed the passers-by would think of the family that lived there, and of their taste.

"It's nobody's business what we have in our yard. People can look the other way if they don't like it."

"It's my business, and I'd get tired of looking the other way all the time."

"Well, you are not going to touch these plants."

"Yes; the plants are going to come up after awhile and are going to be put where they belong."

The doctor's eyes blazed at this calm defiance of his authority.

"I'll raise a d—l of a row if you touch them."

"Very well, dear, *I'll* only raise the cabbage-plants."

"Infinite wrath and infinite despair" chased themselves by turns over the doctor's expressive countenance. He certainly intended that the plants should stay there, because—well—because he had *said* they should, and that ought to be reason enough for her. But he felt so helpless. He seemed to be realizing how very much harder it would be for him to keep the plants in the yard than for her to take them out of it; how very much harder it would be for him to stay away from the office to guard them in person than for her to go out whenever she saw fit and take them up.

Of course, if she would only manifest the proper fear and respect for his authority, the cabbage-plants would be safe wherever he might be; but there seemed to be nothing for him to do but to utter one more threat and stalk away to the office, feeling as he went the impotence of the threat.

When he came home to tea everything was forgotten, and succeeding days were as pleasant as pleasant could be. The doctor would occasionally stroll about the large front yard,—aimlessly, of course,—but his good wife would smile to see that he always cast a covert glance in passing toward the different spots where the cabbage-plants ought to be standing, and they were always there. He began to have some confidence in the efficacy of his commands and threats, and on more than one occasion got his hoe and carefully dug up the grass for the space of a couple of feet around each plant. He was beginning to cultivate them very assiduously.

But there came a day when the doctor's wife went forth with butcher-knife in hand, saying to herself, as she proceeded on her way, "This nonsense will now cease." The plants were taken up, not a vestige of one being left to tell the tale, and transplanted in goodly rows in the garden.

When the doctor came home that evening his wife was singing cheerily in the kitchen. She had noted his approach, and hence she sang,—not the least particle *too* cheerily, not with the slightest exaggeration of indifference nor with a single false note, for any of these things would be detected at a critical moment like that, be accepted as a token of fear and wavering, and subject the citadel to instant storming.

No; this wife sang just as her husband had been accustomed to hear her sing about her work, and she did not realize until afterward what she was singing,—did not know that when her husband appeared on the scene she was singing about hiding till the storm of life is past!

The calm and unterrified demeanor of the singer kept the doctor silent. But who can tell? Perhaps, noting also the words she sang, he felt that here was an unconscious concession to him, and was satisfied. At any rate, not a word of wrath, nor even of reproach, came from his lips. He went out into the garden and looked at the cabbage-plants, came back and spoke very pleasantly about them, and—it was all over.

And, while he would not have confessed it to his wife for worlds, yet he knew, just the same, that the strength of her position lay in the fact that she was in the right. She could afford to be serene and unruffled at the time of his blusterings, and calmly bide her time. And, while he would not have confessed it to his wife for worlds, in his inmost heart he was proud of her for being brave enough to—first being sure she was right—go ahead.

Physicians are sometimes autocrats in another way: they may be too careful of their wives. Have we not gone forth in the joyous spring-time of the year, when the birds were singing in the tree-tops, and all Nature was casting aside her winter garments, swathed in the heaviest of cloaks and wrappings, while with difficulty we lived, and moved, and breathed? Have we not had roaring fires built up for our comfort and enjoyment, against our strenuous protests on spring and autumn days, when only a little fire was needed, which converted our comfortable rooms into hot-houses and caused doors and windows to fly open on every side?

Then, in the morning our husbands are solicitous about our colds, and wonder how we got them. Of course, there is some compensation in being able to tell them how we got them; but they are often a little skeptical, for after building up the fires they go to the office, and by the time they get home the fires have burned low and the opened doors and windows have cooled off the rooms and are closed. But, nevertheless, we know what we know.

There is an attention to little things and a kind care that husbands may exercise over their wives which is always pleasing and grateful to them, but beware lest it be overdone. From a very small volume that lies before me I cull these golden words:—

" There is a medium in all things, even in the manifestation of affection, even in the bestowal of kind attention, even in the removal of little miseries. Devotion does not consist in doing for one *all that can be done*, but simply in doing *all that may be agreeable or useful to him*. . . . As we all passionately love our liberty we hold to our little eccentricities; we do not like to have that arranged with too much order which we naturally leave a little out of order; we would even not have too much *care* taken of us." (The italics are not my own, but are quoted, too.)

And now I would like to add that I am fully aware all doctors are not reprehensible in this matter of being overcareful of their wives. Then, between the too-careful husband and the one who cares nothing about his wife at all, except to be sure that she gets his meals and keeps his buttons sewed on, should be found the happy medium; but if we are not able to find it, by all means give us the overcareful doctor, whose failing at least leans to virtue's side, while the other is fit for treason, stratagems, and spoils. Surely this language is not too strong to apply to him, when Shakespeare could apply it to a man who has no music in his soul.

I HAVE sometimes thought, when reading slowly and delightedly that loveliest of pastorals, "The Deserted Village," that when Goldsmith described the village preacher he was not far from describing the village doctor, too. This may seem at first glance a rather peculiar statement, but let us see:—

"There where a few torn shrubs the place disclose,
The village preacher's modest mansion rose."

The doctor's mansion is almost invariably a modest one, and the "few torn shrubs" are too often partially descriptive of his place.

The physician's wife often has occasion to bewail her lot in not being able to get anything about the yard, the lot, or the garden done when she wants it done. When she mildly suggests that such and such a thing ought really to be done now, the doctor says he's not going to pay out money for that when he has a dozen men already paid to do it.

Well, the doctor's wife is sensible and economical, and she, too, would like very much for the men that are already paid to come, but she has observed that they do not come hurrying to do these things. Once in a while a straggler drops in; but if he get a chance before the day is over to go somewhere else, where he has not been paid, away he goes! And so the few torn shrubs in the doctor's yard are left to their own wild will; the grass, all unacquainted with the mower or the scythe, grows up and flourishes like a green bay-tree; the jimson-weeds in the garden wax exceeding mighty, and the mud-hole in the lot becomes a veritable Slough of Despond.

But then our own and the neighboring children can have fine games of hide-and-seek in the tall grass, we can blow beautiful soap-bubbles through the long blossoms of the jimson, and there seem to be no pilgrims going through our horse-lot, on their way to the Celestial City, to fall into the Slough of Despond, as Bunyan's pilgrim did; and so life has its compensations.

"His house was known to all the vagrant train,
He chid their wanderings, but relieved their pain."

The doctor's house (and office) is well and widely known not only to all the wandering vagrants, but to the fixed vagrants of a community as well. If it is not permissible to speak of *fixed* vagrants, it seems to me it ought to be, for the doctor has ever near him a large and steady clientele of that class.

Sometimes it is a vagrant *mind* which seeks a refuge there. One summer morning several years ago a crazed woman presented herself at our door, and her agonized plea to be permitted to come in and live with us, to escape her persecutors at home and elsewhere, were pitiful to hear. She pleaded long and earnestly, but, finding it could not be, she said she was sick and would like to have some medicine to take home with her; they would not believe she was sick at home, and would not have a doctor nor get her any medicine. The doctor felt her pulse and found it as good as his own, then fixed her up some harmless preparation. He brought it to her, and said, in a very impressive manner, "Now you are to go right home, and take this just as soon as you get there, or it may not do you any good." He put it into her hand and she started immediately, but before reaching the gate she turned and said, "Maybe I'd better come back and take it here, if you think it would be too late after I get home."

The doctor was a little disconcerted at being so nearly caught in his own trap, but only for an instant.

"No, it won't be too late if you go straight and start now."

She opened the gate and closed it behind her and started down the walk at a rapid pace, when she happened to remember something, stopped short, turned and came swiftly back. At the gate she opened the purse she carried in her hand, took out some money and called out, "Doctor, I forgot to pay you for the medicine."

I am glad to say the money was not accepted, but I, who had been a spectator of the scene, felt that no other proof was needed as to the unnatural condition of her mind.

Then once in a great while a crazy person comes to town to consult the doctor about something and just concludes to go down and see the doctor's wife, too. Now doctors' wives are not inhospitable, and yet they cannot rejoice over the advent of lunatic guests. It is hard to entertain lunatics. The topics they converse about are such unusual topics, and there are such sudden and startling changes in their conversation that the poor doctor's wife is put to her wits' ends to know what to say to them. Happily for her it is not often that they come.

One day in mid-winter, when the snow was lying thick upon the ground, a crazy woman came in at the gate, up the walk, and on to the veranda. Then she stopped, took a broom which stood beside the door, and for the space of half an hour, or what seemed like it, vigorously swept her overshoes. This done, she took them off, and then a thundering knock resounded through the house. I advanced into the hall, with heart

palpitating, to admit her. She greeted me pleasantly, and I greeted her as cordially as I could. I saw she carried an old satchel and was almost sure that she had murderous weapons concealed in it, for I had often heard that she had solemn convictions that it was her duty to kill certain persons. A wild fear seized me that she might have a conviction that day that it was her duty to kill the baby cooing so innocently on the bed.

But my visitor took off her bonnet and sat down, and we—conversed. She said she had come to town on purpose to see the doctor, and, after she had left his office, just concluded to give his wife a call, too. Part of her conversation was rational, and we got along very well; then suddenly it would stray off to where I could not follow it, and I would sit dumb. The dinner-hour came before very long, however, and with it came the doctor, to my infinite relief. I invited our guest to come out to dinner with us. Swift as an arrow she sprang from her chair and, with her face almost in mine, she said, "Thank you. I'll be pleased to eat with you."

THE PHYSICIAN'S WIFE.

If I had never known before that she was crazy, I should have known it then, because if she had not been she would have hesitated a little, after the manner of sane people, and said, "Why, no—I guess—not"; and then I should have repeated the invitation and she would have yielded reluctantly and said, as we proceeded to the dining-room, "Now I hope you didn't go to a bit of trouble." And I should have assured her that we did not, while at the same time her practiced eye would have taken in several little signs of extra trouble and been gratified, perhaps, thereby.

But this poor, wandering mind accepted the invitation without demur; its owner ate her dinner with hearty enjoyment and went her way. It may be that sane people may learn from the insane sometimes.

"He chid their wanderings, but relieved their pain."

How often has some wanderer from the paths of peace—of health, morality, and virtue—sought the doctor's counsel and his aid! How gratefully they have received any aid, any relief from pain, bodily or mental! How respectfully they have listened to his chidings, knowing that he spoke from absolute knowledge of absolute facts and their results; have listened while he told them, in no uncertain tones, that the wages of sin and of neglect would surely be paid by death! And when he has solemnly warned them to go and sin no more, how many have gone, yet how few have sinned no more!

> "Unskillful he to fawn or seek for power,
> By doctrines fashioned to the varying hour.
> For other aims his heart had learned to prize,
> More bent to raise the wretched than to rise."

Rarely does a political bee get to buzzing in the doctor's bonnet; and his patients may congratulate themselves that he keeps the even tenor of his way, and leaves these outside and disturbing matters to those more to the manor born.

Among the eighty-eight United States Senators there is only one physician, and it may be that he had retired from medicine before entering

the arena of politics; though as to that **I am not
advised. But** his is an "isolated case."

The doctor is much more inclined **to keep
clear of the** madding crowd **and to do his life-
work in** a quieter way, for "thus **to relieve the
wretched was** his pride."

"A man he was to all the country dear,
And passing rich with forty pounds a year."

I know of no idea more **firmly** implanted **in
the** human mind—at least, in **the** human **mind**
adjacent **to** towns and villages—than **the idea
that the physician is a moneyed** man, **or, at any
rate, never knows** what **it is to need money.
Those** holding **this most erroneous belief have
never been physicians or physicians' wives, nor
relatives of either** physicians **or** their wives, **else
their eyes would long ago have been unsealed,—
indeed, would never have been blinded.**

Only a few days **ago, the doctor of our household was** walking **along the street, when he
stopped to remind a man who owed** him that **he
was needing money; at which the man looked at**

him in unfeigned amazement, and said, in his slow drawl, "Why, my—goodness, Doc., you don't expect *me* to pay you anything!" Then with another amazed look, "*You* don't need money!"

And even among perfectly honest, upright, and well-to-do people there is often thoughtlessness in regard to the doctor's dues. Only thoughtlessness; for if they knew how sorely he is pressed for ready money, at times, they would hasten to settle accounts with him. Just here I would like to pay tribute to that blessed minority who, when a physician's services are ended, pay him for them promptly, ungrudgingly, and uncomplainingly. How like an oasis in the desert they have seemed to him, in the weary march of life! Every physician has some patrons of this kind to keep alive his hope and faith in humanity, but always, as now, perhaps, they will be a minority. One of the brightest and most sensible women of my acquaintance once admitted to me frankly that, while she always wanted to keep every other bill paid up, she had often thought and said that it did not matter much about the doctor's bill; it might go a year or two longer. When a good many people in a community hold the same view, and a good many others pay him in commodities instead of cash, it is not difficult to see what effect it is likely to have on both the doctor and his wife, and upon his wife's toilet. I say his wife's toilet, for, come what may, the doctor's toilet must not suffer greatly. When it becomes necessary for one of the two to dress shabbily for a time, by all means let it be the wife! Otherwise both may have to dress shabbily *all* the time. Of course, the manly doctor will protest against this, and then the wife's common sense must outweigh his sentiment in the matter. She must assure him that it is for their mutual good, and not because she has not a proper regard for herself, or because she thinks, for one moment, that she is less worthy of the best than he. No, not that. Humility, true and unaffected, is one of the loveliest of virtues, and let us hope that every physician's wife knows something of its meaning; but let her never know, for one instant, the meaning of servility toward her husband or toward any living creature.

She will say to her husband, "It is business now that I am talking. I am here at home most of the time, and can afford to do without some things for my toilet for awhile, but you can't; you are a professional man, and you must dress as a professional man."

It is not respectful to the women or the men, to whose homes the physician is summoned, to present himself in untidy or worn-out garments.

All these so-called little things have and ought to have their weight and influence in the community, and the physician who constantly disregards them will come out a loser in the race. So, if the time comes to the physician, as doubtless it has come to most physicians, when he feels that the tide of fortune is ebbing a little, let him not grow careless and indifferent about his personal appearance, as men are prone to do at such times, and cause people to say, "Have you noticed how seedy and shabby Dr. X. is looking lately? He is losing his grip, isn't he?"

That is the very time when he must gird himself for battle with more vigor and care than ever. Then, let the wife wear her seedy, shabby cloak, if need be, for another season or two, and along with it other articles of apparel to correspond,—"the distinguishing badges of the profession," as one physician has jovially put it. What matters it? She has pride,—not more than other wives, I think; not less, I hope; and it will buoy her up until that "good time coming" when shabby garments will no longer be a concomitant of her life. And, in the meantime, she can be looking backward as well as forward for hope and inspiration. Her thoughts can revel in the easy and delightful life physicians' wives must have led once upon a time in the Paradise of Doctors. This paradise is described briefly in a little volume published many years ago.

A distinguished physician of Massachusetts embodied some of his ideas and opinions in a fable, which he called "The Paradise of Doctors." In that golden age, physicians and their wives went with firm and joyous steps along the streets and into establishments where commodities of any and every kind were for sale. They went without money, for they needed none. They exchanged gilded pills for everything purchased,—not with a hesitating or apologetic air, as if they knew in advance that their commodities would be refused or scowled at if accepted, but proudly and confidently, because there was an eager—yes, an insatiate—demand for these gilded pills, and shop-keepers almost fell over each other in their haste to make the exchange. The obligation was all on their side. Beautiful fable!

I am reminded here of a Russian fable, one of Ivan Tourgeneff's, "The Two Virtues," which is not too old, I think, to bear repetition here. I give it in illustration of a point I wish to make:—

One day it occurred to the good god to give a party in his palace of azure. All the virtues were invited, but the virtues only; and in consequence there were no gentlemen among the guests.

Very many virtues, both great and little, accepted the invitation. The little virtues proved to be more courteous and agreeable than the great ones. However, they all seemed thoroughly happy, and conversed pleasantly with one another, as people who are well acquainted, and, indeed, somewhat related, ought to do. But suddenly the good god noticed two fair ladies who seemed not to know each other. So he took one of the ladies by the hand and led her toward the other. "Benevolence," said he, indicating the first,—"Gratitude," turning to the other.

The two virtues were unutterably astonished. For since the world began—and that was a great while ago—they had never met before. The point I wish to illustrate is one that must have fallen under the observation of most physicians and their wives. They have occasion to know that benevolence and gratitude are very often strangers to each other. Physicians have gone through winter's snow and summer's heat, through rain and storm, attending patients, getting nothing, asking nothing, expecting nothing in return. The doctor must pay the druggist for medicines; often he must pay for a livery team; but he gets nothing, for he knows they are absolutely too poor to pay him. It sometimes happens that time brings about a change; that these same patients are lifted from poverty into comfort, and are able to pay all bills of every kind. Does the doctor remind them of former times, and of their indebtedness to him? No; he does not think of such a thing, and they don't think of it either. But when they get sick now they employ him, of course? No; when they get sick now they employ some other doctor! His services cost them nothing in the old days, and hence they put no value upon them now; probably believe that the doctor himself did not consider them worth charging for, since he presented no bill and no duns. I clip the following from a recent paper:—

"Dr. Warren had been in the habit for a number of years of giving professional advice to a lady in reduced circumstances, whom he regarded as hardly able to offer him any compensation. At length she ceased consulting him, and he did not see her for a long time. Finally, happening to meet her on the street, he said to her: 'Why, Mrs. ——, what has become of you? You have not been near me for months.'

"'Well, the fact is, Dr. Warren,' she said, in all simplicity, 'I didn't seem to gain very much, and I thought I'd consult a pay doctor!'"

It has long been a conviction of mine that it would be better for a physician, in all cases, whether he expects to get a cent or not, to make a fair charge and let patients know the amount of his bill, so they may know he values his services at something more than nothing.

Then, there is another form of ingratitude which I am glad to believe is rare. A few nights ago a man presented himself at our door, for whom the doctor has prescribed for years gratuitously, and actually threatened his life if he did not go down to his house. This, after the doctor had explained to him, on the preceding evening, that another physician was paid to do his practice,—employed to do the practice of the poor. But threats are not very potent weapons when used upon a man with any courage, and he calmly replied, "I will not go at all unless you bring me an order from the supervisor." He knew that would settle the matter, as the supervisor would, of course, give him an order upon the other physician.

THE PHYSICIAN'S WIFE. 117

Ingratitude sometimes takes another form. A well-known literary man, writing from his home in London to an American journal, relates an incident which he says has been going the rounds of the English press. It illustrates so well what most physicians and their wives have seen for themselves, that I give it:—

"A gentleman, calling at a friend's house, finds him away from home, and goes into the drawing-room—a newly furnished and splendid apartment—to write a letter to him. The ink-stand, a gorgeous affair with the latest improvements, 'tilts up,' and the whole contents are spilled on the delicate carpet. The visitor rings the bell for a servant, and points to the evidence of his crime. The good-natured maid-servant admits that it does look bad, but says she will do her best to remove it. If she can erase those stains, says the guest to himself, I

will give that good girl five pounds. She brings soap and a bucket of hot water, and presently things begin to look a little better. Perhaps a couple of sovereigns will be sufficient, says the guest to himself. Then, as it gets better and better, he thinks half a sovereign will meet the case. And, at last, when all traces of the accident are removed, he gives her—half a crown."

It happens occasionally in the doctor's experience, when he is confronted with a case so grave as to offer little hope for recovery, that the grief-stricken father or mother, if possessed of means, will say to him, imploringly, "Doctor, if you will save my child I will give you a thousand dollars." The doctor can promise them nothing but that he will do all that is in his power to do. Perhaps on the next morning the patient is a very little better, and the tension begins to loosen just a little. In the evening she is still better, and it is, "Doctor, save her and I will give you five hundred dollars." By morning the danger is considerably lessened. Then it is, "Just get her well and I will give you two hundred dollars." And, finally, when the patient has recovered and the bill is settled, he gets—his usual remuneration—all he asked, and all he really expected.

Of course, in instances like the above, the ingratitude, if it can be justly termed ingratitude, is only natural, and is amusing rather than reprehensible. Thus fades away many a generous impulse when time is allowed for its consideration.

But here it is quite different. It happens, sometimes, that a very urgent and appealing call comes for the doctor to go and perform some difficult surgical operation, or otherwise relieve the sick and suffering. Sometimes the patient is miles away, costing the physician both time and money. But when it is all done, the household is so grateful to him! They say with fervent tones, and mean what they say, "Doctor, I will pay you for this if I have to saw wood for it." Or, sometimes, "Doctor, you shall be paid if I have to wash to pay you." The doctor goes away, the surgical operation has accomplished its purpose, the patient gets better every day, and the grim spectre no longer stares them in the face. Naturally, the fervor of gratitude toward the physician grows less and less as the weeks go by, "decreasing with the square of the distance," until time obliterates it altogether, and this faithful servant does not even get his half-crown.

Still, when an imploring cry for help comes to him, what is he to do? Unless his heart is made of stone, he must find it well-nigh irresistible. When a human being is in dire distress, shall he withhold his helping hand, even though it be extended to a vagabond or thief? No; at times like these he must "forget their vices in their woe." Often it has been with the physician as with the village preacher, that—

"Careless their merits or their faults to scan,
His pity gave ere charity began."

In a conversation with a medical man, some time ago, on matters pertaining to the profession, I inquired if surgery were not more remunerative than other kinds of practice. He smiled a sad smile and shook his head. "That has not been my experience, and I don't believe I will be far wrong to assert that I don't believe it has been the experience of most other practitioners." Quite surprised, I inquired how that could be when the fees for surgery were so good. "Well," said the doctor, "it does seem to me, sometimes, that three-fourths of the people who meet with accidents—who get broken ribs, broken bones, hands mashed, feet cut, etc.—are charity patients."

"That is something new to me. I never heard the theory advanced before that accident is a respecter of persons."

"I suppose an explanation may lie in the fact that it is only the poor, those engaged in the hardest and roughest of work, who are exposed to such dangers."

"Well, I don't know. There isn't much consolation in that for you doctors, but it must be some consolation to the victim that he will, at least, be exempt from a doctor bill. Perhaps, though, if these people stood in fear of doctor bills as well-to-do people do, there would be fewer accidents among them."

Not long after this conversation I was standing at the window (it was toward the close of a dark, rainy day in February), looking out upon a dreary, yet a lovely world. The rain, which was part sleet, had been falling ceaselessly since early morning, and freezing as it fell, till the whole world seemed dressed in silver armor. I had been looking out at the procession of passers-by, and noting with some amusement the efforts of the portly, dignified pedestrians to keep their footing.  One man went down, glanced rapidly around him in every direction, then picked himself up and ambled onward again.

After awhile I turned to the cosy fire, seated myself in a big arm-chair before it, thinking, as I gazed into

its glowing depths, of the icy pavements, and
wondering that there were not a good many
broken limbs on a day like this. Whether I
fell into a light doze, or whether it was only
a day-dream that came to me, I am hardly
able to state, but the procession still kept mov-
ing along, some slipping, some clutching at the
fences or the lamp-posts, or whatever might help
them to keep upon their feet; but now the
greater number were falling and actually break-
ing a leg or an arm as fast as they fell. The
victims were, without exception, well dressed
and apparently well-to-do people, while the
ragged and poverty-stricken passed safely by.
What would have been very serious if only one
man had broken a leg or an arm was irre-
sistibly comical when several dozens were in the
same plight, and those with broken legs sat
there and laughed immoderately, while those
with broken arms, who had picked themselves
up, stood leaning against the fences and laughing, too. (I am sure I must have laughed aloud
in my innocent glee, but I have no recollection

of it.) I saw my husband and all the other doctors of the town come hurrying to the scene, and they, too, looked happy and well pleased, at the same time struggling manfully to look only solemn and professional. As I gazed upon it all and its full significance burst upon me, my thoughts and fancies took on a roseate hue. The worn carpet on the floor became new and soft to the feet; the faded curtains at the windows vanished away, and in their places hung the softest and loveliest of draperies; the two rocking-chairs, which had served their day and generation faithfully and well, were gone, and in their places were two others of more modern style, while a beautiful new cloak came enticingly within my vision. Suddenly I was awakened, or startled, by a loud knock at the door. I sprang from my chair and went to open it, realizing as I went that the lovely conjurings of my dream—or of my fancy—had vanished from the room, and that daylight was fast receding. I opened the door.

"Is the doctor here?"

"No; he hasn't come down yet."

"I thought mebbe I'd find 'im at home, as it's about supper-time."

"I think he will be here in a few minutes; but, perhaps, you had better go to the office, if you are in a hurry."

"Well, I'll go up there, and if I miss 'im tell 'im when he comes that Bill Meechim's fell an' broke 'is leg, and wants 'im to come right down."

I closed the door with a sad, resigned smile, and went back into our dear, shabby, little sitting-room; for well I knew that Bill Meechim paid no bills, whatever such intention his name might imply. Then I sat down and reasoned with myself, and before two minutes had gone by I had convinced myself that I was glad my dream—or day-dream—was not a reality. For the physician's wife is not a malicious creature; she is not even uncharitable as distinguished from the rest of mankind. She doesn't want the well-to-do people in the community to break their bones or otherwise injure themselves, but she cannot help wishing sometimes that more of the people who do fall and get broken bones, etc., were able to pay for being made whole again.

One day, when the doctor of our household had brought down two other physicians to dinner, we had a little talk on this subject of surgery. I happened to remark to the elder physician that it was just about a year ago that the doctor had taken me out to his village to spend the day with his good wife while he assisted the elder physician in amputating a leg, or the lower part of a leg. (I use the term "elder physician" simply to distinguish this doctor from the young doctor who accompanied him.) "Yes," said the elder physician, "and that woman gets around as well now as she ever did, if not better."

"She wears an artificial limb, I suppose?"

"Yes; one that I made for her myself."

"You made it? I didn't know a doctor could do such things. Why didn't she get one ready-made?"

"I wrote to a large firm in Chicago that manufacture artificial limbs, telling them that because of the limb having lain for months in a flexed position on a pillow it had become partially ankylosed." (Dear, unprofessional reader, if any such there be, that only means that the knee-joint had become stiff and refused to extend as it should.) "And she also had bursitis from resting her knee on a chair and crawling around to do her work. They replied that they wouldn't undertake to fit an artificial limb to a stump of that kind unless the woman came up so that they might see it for themselves, and even then they couldn't guarantee entire satisfaction. Well, they are very poor people, and it was simply out of the question for her to go to that expense. Then, the limb would have cost at least seventy-five dollars, and perhaps twice as much; so I just said to myself, 'If they can't do that job, I can.'"

No one knowing the elder physician as I do would doubt for a moment that he could, and I listened in deep admiration to one whose skill in making a patient whole again transcended anything that had ever fallen within my personal knowledge.

"I made a plaster cast of the leg, which was about this shape":—(1)

"Then, in order that the foot should accommodate itself to the flexed condition of the knee, I had it made so that the whole thing looks like this":—(2)

"You see, the village blacksmith, the shoe-maker, the harness-maker, and I put our heads together, and the result is an artificial limb."

"But where is the foot?" said I, looking at the drawing.

"I haven't got the foot made yet, but I am going to make it. She walks on a block now."

"Well, great are the resources of the country doctor!" said I, laughing.

"The half has never been told about the country doctor yet," replied the elder physician, with a smile.

"Let me see," said the young doctor, "didn't you get your idea, or one similar to it, from Tom Jones's mule?"

The elder physician turned his mild eyes upon the young doctor in gentle rebuke for insinuating that he could draw his idea from *a mule*, as if he were a mere veterinary surgeon!

"Tell us about the mule," said I, on the *qui vive* in an instant.

"Oh, it isn't much to tell; only I guess Tom got his start in the world through that mule. He's a rising young lawyer in one of our large cities now, you know, but then he was a poor country boy. He had a fiddle that he had paid a quarter for, but he came across a fellow that had more music in his soul than he had, I guess; for one day I met  him leading this young mule colt, which was a cripple,—had one of its fore-feet doubled under.

"'Hello! Tom. What are you going to do with that mule?' I said.

"'I traded my fiddle for him and got a dollar besides,' said Tom, proudly. Then, seeing my eye bent on the doubled-under foot, he said, 'Do you suppose he'll ever be good for much?'

"'Well, I don't know; but—I'll tell you—suppose you take him to the blacksmith and have him put a brace on that foot. Have him nail it to the bottom of the hoof, then turn the foot up as far as he can and fasten the brace up on the leg; then you keep tightening it a little every day, and we'll watch him and see what effect it will have. I believe it will help him.'"

"Did it really straighten out the foot, Doctor?" I asked, deeply interested.

"It made it all right. Tom sold the mule after awhile for a hundred dollars, which gave him a start toward his education."

And so the cunning brain and philanthropical heart of this one country doctor caused an unfortunate brute to walk instead of limp through life; it gave a poor boy his start in the world; it caused a poor woman, who must otherwise have gone through life on crutches, to walk once more as she had done of old. Truly, the half *has* never been told of the country doctor.

As one of the trio of medical men remarked that day, he must rise superior to circumstances; he must not recognize the impossible.

I did not hear the elder physician express himself on this point, but it is more than probable that *he* paid the harness-maker and the blacksmith and the shoe-maker for their work upon the artificial limb, and it is also probable that he himself received nothing.

After he was through with his little experience the young doctor remarked that that was a first-class case of talipes equinus, and then went on to say, " By the way, I was called to see a case of talipes calcaneus the other day, which I treated by tenotomy. How does that strike you?" appealing to each of his elders in turn.

" Well, said the elder physician," that might do very well, but I would prefer a plaster-of-Paris dressing."

" If the child was very young, massage and molding the foot might be employed with good results. I believe I would prefer that, or adhesive plaster," said the other physician.

"Where doctors disagree, what shall the laity do," thought I.

Then this same doctor spoke of a case of lordosis he had once had, and this physician had been driven to the conclusion that it was due to malposition of the acetabula rather than to tuberculosis vertebrarum.

And so the talk went on. I only sat in wonder, and still the wonder grew how three small heads could carry all they knew.

My little boy came into the room pretty soon, saying, as he advanced toward me, "Mamma, what is the matter with my lip; it hurts?"

I scrutinized the lip carefully, and then, seeing that the doctors had ceased talking and were observing us, I replied, with deep satisfaction and triumph, "Why, dear, you have a very mild case of herpes labialis."

My boy was disgusted and indignant, and felt that he had been imposed upon by his own mother. Two of the doctors looked a little surprised, and one of them greatly amused, while I was only happy that once upon a time I had learned that a cold sore or a fever-blister bore this high-sounding Latin term, and that I had remembered it and could employ it now in very self-defense.

Then the polysyllables and the surgery were dropped, and I had a chance to inquire if a case of choking or strangling ever disconcerted either of our medical guests, or caused them to hurry the least bit in answer to a summons. My inquiry was based upon the fact that only the day before, while we sat at dinner, a young fellow had come breathlessly into the house, saying, "Doctor, come quick, my uncle is strangling!"

"Is that so?" said this calm doctor, sitting perfectly still. "Was he eating anything at the time?"

"I don't know," said the agitated messenger, looking helplessly at the motionless form of the doctor.

"Well, I'll be down," said the latter, as he turned quietly toward his plate again.

Then, in low, but intensely-earnest tones, I said, "Oh, do get your hat and *go!*"

The doctor rose and went with his usual **gait away.** While he was gone I recalled what he had once told me about a little boy who had come in a panic of fright to his office to get him to come quickly, for the baby was choking to death. "All right; go back home, and I'll come," he said.

He waited on one or two patients who were in the office, then started to see the choking baby. He had not proceeded far when he saw the figure of the little boy, who was running to meet him, and a happy voice piped out, "The baby's unchoked!" "Is it?" said the doctor. "Well, I knew it would be unchoked, my boy."

I thought, too, of my own baby boy, who, a good many years before, had sat in his little chair playing with a large, stiff-paper butterfly. By and by there was a terrible gagging and choking, and, looking into his mouth, I saw the butterfly, or a large portion of it, pressed flat against the back of the throat. Frightened beyond the power to move, I screamed for the girl to run for the doctor. She stood not on the order of her going, but went at once, over the back paling and across "the branch," not stopping to go around by the gate; for she, too, loved the baby, and she, too, was white and breathless. In another minute I saw her flying form returning over the fence as it had gone, and honored and blessed her for it! After a little I saw the doctor coming,—not over the paling, as that blessed girl had done, and as he would come if he loved the baby as we did, but leisurely sauntering down the walk the longest way he could possibly take, and with him another physician who

had happened to be chatting with him in the office when the summons came. To be a witness to that leisurely gait, and see how absorbed the two doctors were in their conversation, which was evidently of a pleasing nature, was to fill my soul with wrath. To be sure, the butterfly had come forth just after the girl departed, and the baby was now kicking his heels against the chair in high glee; but how was he to know that? I met him with a stony glance when at last he got in—but in the midst of my ruminations the doctor returned from the strangling uncle and resumed his dinner. He remarked, after awhile, that the strangling was all over with before that boy got here, of course. He knew that when he came.

"Well; when the boy was so frightened, it was agony to him and to me to see you so immovable."

The two medical guests admitted that they had never been particularly agitated over cases of that kind, because really very few people ever had choked or strangled to death. Then the talk drifted off on to the subject of doctors' bills.

This subject of doctors' bills is a great one, and physicians' wives naturally have much interest in it. To me it has always been an absorbing theme, and often an amusing one. I knew a

The Doctor's Bill.

lady once who was fond of quoting to a physician that old saw about the three degrees in a doctor's comparison: Positive, ill; comparative, pill; superlative, bill. I happened to remember one day that one of the grammars we used in school, when I was a girl, had four degrees of comparison, and so I told her that I could change that and she would like it better still: Diminutive, ill; positive, pill; comparative, kill; superlative, bill; still keeping the bill in the superlative degree, as I knew that would please her. The general public will always say the bill is in the superlative degree. The general public, as we have seen, will also do their part toward keeping it in the subjunctive mood and in the future tense. When Shylock was pleading in fair Portia's court for an abatement of his hard sentence, he said, "You take my house when you do take the prop that doth sustain my house. You take my life when you do take the means whereby I live."

There are a few Shylocks in every community to say to the doctor, by word or act, you take my life-blood when you do take your doctor bill. Yes; some people regard the doctor as a sort of gigantic mosquito let loose upon the community to draw its life-blood. The mosquito has the best of the comparison, for he has only to sing a little while and then present his bill to have it met with assiduous attention; while the doctor often has to whistle for his, whistle long and loud, and then have no attention paid to him at all. It has been said that the doctor's bill, when paid, is often paid in chips and whetstones. I do not just now recall any whetstones that have been brought to us. Perhaps they have come; but as I seldom use a *bona fide* whetstone, I have not noticed them. (It is said that if there is one thing Satan has not succeeded in finding out with certainty, it is a woman's whetstone.) But I can certify to the chips; they have come like angel's visits, few and far between. Bean-poles and big green back-logs have been brought to us, too. The bean-poles were usually too short, but then the back-logs were usually too long; so things were equalized. But when one of these great logs gets to burning well and to "singing again the imprisoned songs of the forest," and after awhile, when it falls into a bed of glowing coals and one can sit within its ruddy light and meditate and dream, she can be very happy there. Then after awhile the children bring in the pop-corn. It is good pop-corn. The doctor said it ought to be good, and it is. He came wearily home with it one day, and as he set the sack down he said, "That ought to be good; it cost me twenty-six dollars and a broken buggy."

There is a bunch of brooms standing in a certain corner at our house. They are very handy and very useful things. We can always get a new broom when we want it, and new brooms sweep clean. The doctor made a good many trips to see a patient two or three years ago, long and tedious trips, for which he had to hire a livery team. But then we got the brooms, and we are soon to get another bunch, I understand; and if we only live long enough, that bill may yet be liquidated.*

We have two patchwork quilts fast hastening on to their final dissolution, one of which cost nine dollars and the other ten. That is pretty expensive, but I like to look on the bright side, and it is better quilts than nothing. (I will add,

---

* Several months have gone by since the above was written, and the second bunch has not arrived yet. By the time the last bunch gets here, I shall be as old as "She."

however, that I don't like to look on the bright side of those quilts and always put them on the bed wrong side up.)

Then we have had, at long intervals, a mess of beans or beets or turnips, or a little bucket of pickles in the brine. We have had soft soap and an occasional load of sand; an occasional load of corn, too, which we needed to feed to the pigs that came on a doctor's bill.

The pigs that we have received in that way have always made me think of a character in "Our Mutual Friend." Of Sloppy it is said that there was too much of him lengthwise, too little of him breadthwise, and too many angles of him anglewise. But Sloppy's redeeming trait was his good heart, and the pigs' redeeming trait was their appetite; so they got beyond the point, after awhile, where they could get through every fence on the premises, however impervious the fences were thought to be.

I was about to say something of the horses and cows that have been taken in on doctors' bills, but there is so little I could say!—unless it might be to assure the reader that, while they have never been conspicuous for youth and beauty, they have been conspicuous for other qualities. I see them now as they file slowly past my mental vision, and drop the veil.

Book-agents are not without their good points. The trouble is, people are uninclined to talk with them long enough to find the good points out. Occasionally a book-agent who owes the doctor comes around and offers to pay him something. If the doctor will just put his name down on his list,—for the influence it will exert, of course,—he will furnish him one of the books on his bill. So the doctor's library is sometimes enriched in this way by a volume it never would have contained otherwise, and which remains, in undisturbed repose, upon the shelf.

Once we had a cane-mill brought to us by a man who owed the doctor. I suppose the doctor looked upon it as quite an accession in the way of personal property, but I felt quite helpless in its presence. I knew the doctor would have neither time nor patience to bother with it, and *I* didn't know how to run it. Besides, if I had known how, we had nothing to put into it to grind, for we had been in the habit of buying our molasses ready-made, and had never raised cane —except in those transitory domestic disturbances which are liable to beset the average household, and then we had spelled it differently. As I stood and gazed upon it my thoughts went back to when I was a little girl, and to the lovely amber compound we used to get from the grocery-store, which was labeled "Golden Syrup." So good and thick it was that, as it wound its slow length from the spigot, the clever and veracious grocer who stood waiting would assure the customer that, upon his honor, you could wind a gallon of it around a knife. The flavor of that golden syrup came as I stood to haunt my palate. And I remembered to have heard the assertion made that it was probably made from cast-off boots and shoes. Childhood is credulous, and I accepted the theory, but the beautiful golden color was always a mystery to me. But, by the time the doctor's family is through with their boots and shoes there is nothing left for any purpose,—unless it be to mulch the grape-vines in the garden.

Then I bethought me of a remote farm-house where, once upon a time, the hostess had passed me a glass tumbler with a peculiar-looking compound in it, and asked me if I would have some of the persimmon molasses. I really didn't know whether I would or not; but curiosity got the better of me, and I dipped out a very small portion. It was not so bad as it might have been.

But at the time our cane-mill came the persimmons were not yet ripe, and I did not like to warp and pucker the good old machine out of all semblance of itself by grinding them in it then. So there seemed to be nothing to do but to let the faithful old servant—which had for years performed its allotted task in the world, doing a little extra service now and then, perhaps, in the way of amputating an arm or a hand or a finger, yet still extracting much sweetness from life as it went—fall into disuse, to rust and decay. For I knew we could never sell it, and there would be no way of getting rid of it,—unless we could pay a doctor bill with it; and physicians are exempt from doctors' bills. That is one bright spot on their horizon. The only way was closed to us, and so it stayed. It is a long time since it was brought to us, and it came upon me rather startlingly, not long ago, that I had seen no traces of it for some time. Perhaps some poor deluded thief in the night has stolen it away from us, or perhaps it has shared the fate of the "one-hoss shay," and gone to pieces,

"All at once and nothing first,
Just as bubbles do when they burst."

Yes; doctors' bills is a great theme; and if I seem to linger long upon it, it is only because justice cannot be done it in few words. It is a subject constantly before the public gaze. One cannot pick up a newspaper without seeing numerous adjurations to the people to avoid doctor bills by taking so-and-so and using so-and-so. (They are to avoid Scylla and choose Charybdis, but this they do not know till after taking.) Would that that part of the public which devours these flaming advertisements, headed by the faces of brilliant and benignant personages only anxious to benefit their fellow-mortals, as a glance at their pictures will reveal, could realize that it is these same considerate advertisers who are fleecing the dear people and carrying off their money, while the regular and legitimate practitioner rarely has more than a good living, and often not that; and this after years of faithful and conscientious study and preparation and the expenditure of hundreds, and often thousands, of dollars! Would that they might stop to ask themselves how many physicians they have ever known, or ever heard of, who got rich from the practice of medicine alone, and hence from these same doctors' bills! Would they be willing to live in a community without physicians? Let us suppose a case,—a very improbable case, it is true, but it will answer our purpose. Let us suppose, then, that the announcement should suddenly be made, in any given community, that all the physicians in the region round about were going to move away, and that no others would ever come in to take their places. I think there would be much consternation and alarm there, and that both friends and foes to the doctors would meet on common ground in imploring them to remain. Finding their entreaties vain, I think the whole community would very shortly be bereft of its inhabitants. They would go, too, and settle near these bugbear doctors, and place themselves in voluntary jeopardy from their bills. There is something a little inconsistent in all this.

Sometimes the physician's wife meets some interesting people, who come to the house to consult the doctor when they do not find him at the office, or to do odd jobs about the place, or to bring something to him or to his wife, when they wish to partially liquidate an old debt; and though the astute doctor knows that these things are often in the nature of a conciliation before contracting a new debt, yet the bird in the hand is always acceptable to him.

There is old Uncle John,—an illiterate, uncouth-looking old fellow, but with a certain courtliness in his manner and in his slow-spoken words very pleasant to hear and see. One gray day in the autumn he knocked at our door, and when I opened it he said, " Good morning, madam; I have brought a load of punkins for the doctor, and I don't jist know where to put 'em."

" Well, I hardly know, either; didn't the doctor tell you where he wanted them put?"

" Yes; he said somethin' about the oats-house, but I wanted to be sure of the right place for 'em. I looked in the oats-house, and they's two or three little rooms in there."

"Well, I'll go out with you and see about it."

Reaching the oats-house, I peer around its dusty interior, and, finally, make up my mind that here in this little room is where the doctor probably wanted the pumpkins put; and Uncle John, too, thinks it is likely that is the place. (The doctor kindly, but firmly, let me know, when he came home that night, that that was *not* the place.)

"I'll jist move this wi-er out of the way," says Uncle John, as he lifts a coil of barbed wire and deposits it in a corner.

I go to the wagon and take a look at the pumpkins, and one glance leads me to ask: "Is the doctor getting these for cow-feed, Uncle John?"

"Well, I don't rightly know what he wants

with 'em; but I owed 'im, and I thought I'd bring 'im a load."

The cow refused point-blank to have anything to do with them when they were offered to her for her evening meal; which astonished the doctor, and made him feel that he did not rightly know what he wanted with them, either.

"But what is that queer-looking thing over there in the corner?" as my eye falls on an object which, from its size, shape, and color, looks like it might be a cross between a red sweet-potato and a ripe cucumber.

"That! why, that's a—I don't know what *is* the right name for it, but *we* call it a—" (he mentioned a name that has hopelessly gone from my memory, and it seems no amount of coaxing can bring it back). Then he took out his knife, opened it slowly, and cut the object in question in two pieces, scraped off a little, and handed it to me.

"Taste it, madam; it's good."

I did so. It tasted a good deal like a gourd.

"When that is cut in rings and baked, I

wouldn't change it for any sweet-potater that ever growed."

I thought it probable that Uncle John was not a *connoisseur* in culinary matters, but only asked him if he had ever raised any "cushaws."

"Any which?"

"Cushaws; at least, that's what I have always heard them called. I mean those crook-necked squashes that make such good pies."

"Oh, yes! Well, I used to raise 'em a long time ago when I first come out to the perraries, but the soil is gettin' woren out, an' I don't try to raise 'em any more. They ought to have a purty rich soil."

"I haven't seen any of them for a long time. I'm very fond of them."

"You've got a nice little garden-spot in there, I sees. Git ye some seeds next year, an' have Doc. raise ye some"; which kindly advice causes me to smile,—an involuntary and knowing smile. Uncle John does not know that the gardening at our house is done principally by "Doc.'s" wife, with a little spasmodic help from a man or a boy who is "already paid," and she knows too well what that means.

"I've got to go 'round to the picter-gallry when I git through hyer," says the old man, presently.

"Going to have some pictures taken?"

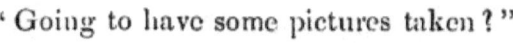

"Why, I dunno; but I reckon they're already tuk. I was in thar the last time I come to town axin' about it. I axed the man how long it 'ud take to git my shadder struck and how much he'd charge to do it. He sot me down in a big green cheer, and told me he'd see about it. Then he got a consarn, with legs to it and a blankit over it, out thar in front ov me, and put a grabbin' machine behind my hed. I'd never been in jist such a fix before, madam, for I never had no picters tuk before, and I was gettin' pretty bad skeered. Then he told me to set right still and look at a hole in the wall, and look pleasant."

"Well, you did look pleasant, I am sure, Uncle John."

"I was feelin' mighty onpleasant, madam; but I tried my level best, and fetched the biggest smile I could fetch, and jist then he jerked the blankit off, and then throwed it over the machine again and said he was done with me."

"You felt glad it was over with, didn't you?"

"My! but I couldn't 'a stood it any longer. I'd 'a jist busted right out in another secont."

"Why, Uncle John, I never found it so hard as all that to have a picture taken."

"Mebbe you're longer-winded than me, madam. I never was much good at holdin' my breath; I can't stand it."

The good old man had actually been holding his breath all the while! I tried to picture to myself the expression his face would wear in the photograph, with the "grabbin' machine" scaring him from the rear and the "smile" he had "fetched" when in imminent peril of "bustin' out," and, as soon as I could get my voice under control, I explained to Uncle John that it was not necessary for him to hold his breath at all, and added: "Now, when you go around to the gallery to get your pictures it may be that you won't like them; and if you see anything wrong with them, just sit down in the chair and tell the photographer that you are going to try it again. It will be easier this time."

"All right, madam; I'll jist do that."

The conversation has taken such a friendly turn that Uncle John tells me now he can remember seeing me, when I was a little girl "'bout so high," standing by the gate under the locust-tree, and looking out between the planks of the fence when he would drive up to the old shop.

The old shop! How often in recent years, in passing along the street which led past it, I had paused to look lovingly at its time-stained and smoke-blackened shingles, and to see again in memory some of the busy scenes enacted there so long ago!

"The old shop is gone, now, Uncle John; torn away last year, to make room for newer and better ones."

"There'll never be a better workman in 'em than the boss of the old shop."

I thank the old man in my heart for those words.

> "It matters not what one may do
> To make a nation or a shoe;
> For he who works an honest thing
> In God's pure light ranks as a king."

And musing on the idleness and frivolity in the world, and on the dignity of self-respecting, honest labor, the old man, the wagon, and the gray autumn day all fade from my sight, and in their place there comes the early twilight of a summer day. Far off and faint I hear the anvils ringing, the dumb metal stricken into melody by powerful hammers in the powerful hands of the workmen. A little girl stands—oh, gracious permission!—with upstretched hands and blows the bellows. Never before had that sweet privilege been granted her. She does not know that it is granted now because the stress of the day's work is over and they are closing up for the night. And so she "pumps fire," and her little heart is radiant with happiness; she is helping her father and the men with their work! When her father smiles down upon her, and tells her

"That will do, now," she starts eagerly toward the door, to run home and tell her mother about it, and almost runs against an elegant-looking gentleman standing just inside the door, which covers her with confusion. The gentleman has a white lily in his hand, and he offers it to the shy, homely little girl, who is more confused than ever, for it is not often that anybody notices her at all. And he has spoken so pleasantly, and asked her to stop and chat with him a minute, and has given her, besides, a beautiful flower! The fragrance of the lily and of the kindly impulse have lingered with her through many years, and is around and about her now.

Her reverie is broken by a voice, which says:—

"Now that, madam, is jinerally a monstrous sweet punkin."

She looks across the wagon, now emptied of its load, at old Uncle John, who stands with the golden globe poised upon his hand.

"That does seem to be a pretty nice one. Please put it over in the yard for me; the cow can't have that one."

The old man does so. Then comes back and closes the door of the oats-house, fastens it carefully, climbs into the wagon, and, with a bow and a pleasant "Good-day, madam," drives away.

I go into the house, where I have left the lady who is visiting with us for a few days, and tell her that I have enjoyed a treat. She knows that I have been standing out in the lot, talking to an uncouth-looking old man unloading pumpkins, and smiles. She does not know that I have been caught up to a Delectable Mountain, from whence, like Christian of old, I have had a glimpse into Paradise; only, the Paradise that Christian saw lay just before him, while mine lay more than a quarter of a century behind me,— the Paradise of childhood, which never comes again except in fleeting visions.

Then, there is old Jerry,—as quaint a figure as one might hope to see. I heard a gentleman say, not long ago, that he wished the Hoosier poet could hear old Jerry talk. The Hoosier poet could make him famous by his imitative powers, whereas pen and ink are powerless to portray the peculiarity of his language, as well as of his utterance. There are a good many words in old Jerry's vocabulary that are new to me, and the meaning of some of them is quite beyond my grasp, but that makes him none the less interesting. He comes to our house occasionally. Once he brought me a gallon of blackberries; and, seeing the doctor at home, he came in with the remark, "Doctor, I've been havin' a purty hard pain in hyar," describing with his hand a circle large enough to include several vital organs; "I wish you'd see if you kin cal'late the reason uv it."

"All right," says the doctor, getting up and going toward the old man. He lays his hand with some pressure within the territory indicated by old Jerry. "Does it hurt there?"

"Not a great much."

"Well, does it hurt here?" changing the position of his hand a little.

"Oh, a leetle."

The doctor presses a little harder in another spot.

"Look out, Doc.! It's touchous right thar!"

"Is it?" says the doctor, with as unsmiling and accustomed an air as if that word had been found in the bright lexicon of his youth, and in all the other lexicons he had consulted since his youth. "Then we'll try another place." And he lays his hand with still stronger pressure in another spot.

"*Look out! It's touchouser thar!*"

The doctor says, presently, "I don't believe

there's very much the matter in there. I think you'll be all right in a day or two."

And old Jerry goes away, satisfied.

Another day he came down "for to get that thar fox's skin, Mrs. Fi-er-ball, that the doctor was a-wantin' me to tan fer 'im."

Yes; we had a beautiful red fox-skin which I wanted sent to a taxidermist to be made into a rug, but the doctor said old Jerry could fix it up all right, and then it would be already paid for; which, being quite a consideration, I yielded, though with some misgivings as to old Jerry's artistic abilities. But he comes for the fox-skin. It is a real delight to me to talk to the old man, or, rather, to hear him talk; so I have him sit down, and ask him all manner of questions about the fox-skin, and he enters into a minute description of the process of tanning. After awhile he says: "Well, I reckon I had better be a-movin' to-*wards* home. My ole woman is ailin', an' mebbe she'll want sumpthin."

"What seems to be the trouble?"

"Oh, I don't know. I guess she hain't much sick; but jist sort o' befigged like."

Not knowing what condition one must be in to be "befigged," I did not know what to say; so wisely said nothing.

The old man went on: "Ye see, last Chewsday—now was it a Chewsday or a Wensdy? It was a Wensdy; that's when it was. Well, last Wensdy she seemed to be a-feelin'—no, it wasn't; it was a Chewsday. I know now, because Bill an' me went a-huntin' that day. Well, anyway, she seemed to be feelin' as peart as common ontil along in the evenin', an' then she become fer to be chilly. It was a-rainin' considerable when she went out to milk the cows, but she got 'em milked, an' come in an' got supper an' washed up the dishes, an' then she tuk an agerin' fit onto her, an' sot thar by the fi-er an' agered fer—well, I reckon it must 'a been fer nigh about an hour, and she's been a-agerin' off an' on ever sence."

I quietly inquired why he or Bill didn't milk the cows that rainy evening. Old Jerry looked at me, quite surprised. Evidently, such a thing had never entered his head.

"Why, me and Bill don't never milk. The old woman always does the milkin'. But I must be a-gittin' home, now. I'll bring your skin back as soon as I git it tanned."

Several weeks later he brought it back,—a sight to behold! He said "It isn't as good a job as it mought 'a been, because I've been sort of bumfuzzled lately and not good fer much." I knew nothing of the nature or symptoms of bumfuzzlement, and the doctor was not able to enlighten me; but I felt, in a dim way, that old Jerry ought to be forgiven. The rug, which was to adorn the floor of my spare chamber, lies hidden away from mortal eyes. But, then, the work was already paid for.

Life is like a garment: turn it, and the other side is quite different. We have been looking at the humorous side of some small lives; let us not forget that they have a pathetic side, too, and often it is deeply pathetic. A century and a half ago, one, strolling thoughtfully through an old English church-yard, saw so clearly the pathetic side to lives long before gone out that he was inspired by it to write the most perfect poem in our language. And in that poem he has said :—

> "Let not ambition mock their useful toil,
> Their homely joys and destiny obscure;
> Nor grandeur hear with a disdainful smile
> The short and simple annals of the poor."

Illy, indeed, have I written, if in these short "annals of the poor" I have provoked a single *disdainful* smile. Poverty, in itself, is a weary thing. It bows the heart and dulls the brain; and when with it are linked sickness and misfortune, we have a gaunt and fearful trio. The physician's wife sometimes has occasion to see this other side of life, and to become very thoughtful about it.

Some bright morning in April, when the air is delightful, the birds are singing, and all nature seems as happy as they, she gets into the carriage with her husband and starts out for a drive. The doctor tells her to get all the pleasure she can out of the trip, because he will not get anything out of it. Of course, the doctor does not mean to insinuate that it would naturally be more of a pleasure for his wife to ride with him than for him to ride with her; he only means that he will not get any money out of it.

"It is all charity work to-day, but the roads are good, and I think I can be back at the office in less than three hours."

"When you get back," says the wife, "you will probably find that you have missed one or two good calls."

"Oh, yes; that often happens. It does make a fellow feel out of sorts sometimes to get back from a trip that doesn't pay him a cent, to find that some good patron has gone to another physician in his absence. But, then, we all have the same experience."

"Doctors, then, never feel any elation in getting each other's patients? I mean in getting them in that way."

"What's the use to feel elated? We all

know that people are very apt to go back to their own family physician."

"Yes, when they have their own family physician. It seems to me it used to be the custom, more than at present, for people to have a family physician, and *always* go to him in sickness."

"Well, whether or not it makes much difference about the doctors, it is always a great pleasure to practice for people who really want you, and believe in you. It is so refreshing to find people anxious to do as you say, and not all the time advancing theories of their own as to the efficacy of this mode or that mode of treatment, or of these or those medicines."

"That reminds me of questions I have sometimes been asked because I am a doctor's wife, and therefore ought to know. When Mrs. Y.'s little child was sick she told me what the doctor was doing, and said she did not like it at all. You were not their doctor, my dear, or her complaints would have been made to some other woman. She asked me what I thought about the treatment. I told her that I knew nothing whatever about it, but that all my life I had thought the best thing to do was to obey the attending physician's instructions to the letter, and that I wanted all the responsibility to rest upon him, as I did not feel able or willing to shoulder it myself. I saw that my words had made a favorable impression, and then added, quietly, and a little slyly, 'Of course, the physician may not know any more about it than I do; perhaps not as much; but I cannot help remembering that he has had every *chance* to know more; that he has given years of study to sickness and disease, and ought to know more; and so I let him take the responsibility.''

By and by they reach the little house where the doctor is to make his first call, and, as the sun is beginning to beat down pretty fiercely, his wife concludes to go in to escape from its rays for awhile.

A young girl, perhaps fourteen or fifteen years of age, tosses deliriously upon a miserable bed. She calls continuously for her mother, who is beside her, but she does not seem to know it.

THE PHYSICIAN'S WIFE. 167

The father, looking stolid and indifferent, sits in the farther part of the room. The doctor, who has been attending the patient for several days, finds her fever much higher than he had expected this morning, and turns sharply to the mother, "Have you given those powders just as I told you?" "Yes—that is, I give 'em like you said till her fever begun to come up, and then some of the neighbors said they ought to be stopped, or they'd make her worse."

"*The devil they did!*"

The doctor's eyes blaze, and the poor, tired woman hastens to tell him, in a trembling way, that she only wanted to do what was right, and that, when they told her she ought not to give the powders when the girl had fever, she was worried and didn't know what to do.

"Now, listen to me," says the doctor. "Do what *I* tell you to do. If you are not going to give that girl a chance to get well, it is no use for me to waste my time in coming out here. I haven't the time to throw away. It's going to be a hard pull if she gets through if we do the best for her that we possibly can. Now, are you going to obey instructions, or do you want me to quit coming?"

The poor, harassed woman replies, with quivering voice, "I'll do exactly what you tell me, Doctor, from this on, and you'll see that I will."

As they start away the doctor's wife, who is a mother, too, pauses by the other mother's side long enough to say, very gently, that she hopes her daughter will soon be better, and sees the grateful tears spring to the tired woman's eyes. When they are in the buggy, and have started on, the doctor points to a poor, shaggy-looking cow standing in the field near by.

"There's the cow they promised me if I'd see this case through; but they'll forget all about it, or else they'll tell such a pitiful story that I'll tell them to keep her."

And the wife—thinking of the abject poverty within and without, and that if the cow is taken the three little children peeping at them from behind the house will suffer most of all—inwardly

says I hope they will never pay it, if it has to be paid in that way. Outwardly she says, cautiously feeling her way to see how far it is well to go, "Doctor, I don't think you did quite right, just now."

"What about?"

"Speaking so harshly to that poor woman."

He admits that he is a little ashamed, but what is a man to do in such cases? Besides, the end justifies the means, and it had the desired effect.

"Yes; but it is the principle I am thinking of. I believe in having the 'punishment fit the crime,' whoever is the perpetrator, except that if there is any leniency it ought to be exercised toward the weak and the ignorant."

"Go on. I have been thinking of taking a course of lectures, anyway."

"Well, then, if you had a patient in that fine farm-house yonder, and the lady of the house had done exactly the same thing that that poor woman did, would you have spoken to her in exactly the same way?"

"Well—I don't know. It isn't very likely that she would have done a thing like that."

"You evade the question, I see; but I know what you would have done. You would have told her, in a firm but courteous way, that the patient would have been better if the medicine had been given as directed, and that it is not giving the doctor a fair chance not to follow his instructions, etc. Come, confess now; wouldn't you?"

The doctor smiles at this close questioning; then says, "I'd be able to see a bill at the end of that case, you know."

"Exactly. It is *only* the principle I am talking about. Now, I wouldn't want you to talk to the mistress of the elegant house exactly as you did to the other; that wouldn't be good business; but I don't want you to talk so savagely to the poor and ignorant woman, either. I think you could have attained the same end by gentler means."

The lecture, which both have really enjoyed, is cut short here. They are approaching a little house where a woman stands at the gate evidently waiting for the doctor.

"I seen ye go past awhile ago, Doctor, and watched for ye as ye went back."

"What is the trouble?"

"I wish ye'd come in and see the folks here. They're in an awful bad shape."

"Have they had any doctor waiting on them?"

"No, sir; they sent for two different doctors two or three days ago, but neither one of 'em would come unless they sent the money first, and they couldn't send it, for they hain't got a cent in the house."

The doctor hands the reins to his wife, gets out of the buggy, takes his case, and goes in. After awhile he comes out, looking very sober, and they resume their way for a few minutes in silence. Then he speaks.

"I am glad you didn't see what I have just seen."

"Why, was it so bad?"

"One filthy bed; a man, desperately sick

with pneumonia, lying upon it; his wife, in the last stage of consumption, lying beside him; and a little girl, six or seven years old, with pneumonia, at the foot. I am used to hard sights, but I don't often see anything so bad as that."

The doctor's wife shudders and hides her face in her hands for a moment, as if to shut out the awful picture.

"Is there nobody to do anything for them?"

"Nobody but the neighbors, and they are miserably poor, too, and have their own work to do at home."

The sunshine has lost part of its brilliance for the doctor and his wife, and they drive on in silence, both lost in meditation on the things that are, and, to their finite vision, ought not to be.

A drive of two miles brings them to the other objective point of the trip, and together they enter the little room,—so poor, so bare, and yet so clean. Here the patient is a little child, and a very sick child it is. The mother sits with the baby in her arms, looking down with ineffable love and tenderness into the little face, all unconscious of her gaze, while her toil-hardened hand rests now and again upon the fevered brow.

When the visit has been paid and they are well on their homeward way, the thoughts of the doctor's wife still linger in the little room, where very soon the angel with the amaranthine wreath will come. There is a look on the face of the patient, overworked mother, bending so tenderly over her helpless child, that she will not forget; and in the light of what she has seen this day, the little services and contributions that have come to the doctor, in honest payment of a debt that is so hard to pay, have lost their mirth-provoking power, and touch her now to a remorseful silence.

THERE comes a time in the physician's life when he pauses to take a retrospective view. He has been sitting quietly at home, after a day of hard work and little pay, thinking over some of the hardships of his life. He realizes, all too well, that his youth is slipping away from him, and, with it, much of his manly strength and vigor. He remembers the time when he could lose two or three nights of sleep in succession, and still be able to get through his work without being absolutely tired out. He cannot do that now. There is so much of sickness and suffering and want in the world that it seems he *must* minister to, with no hope of reward,—since his heart has not been made of stone,—and yet, is it fair to his wife and children that he should give so much of his time and his strength to other people? It grieves his kind heart to think that the time may come when he is no longer here to help them, when the little property he has been able to accumulate will not be sufficient for their support; his children will not be educated as he has longed to educate them, and perhaps the wife must work for their daily bread. The thought is agony, and he vows within himself that from this time on he will work for his own family; that he will no longer be a slave to the beck and call of those who will not pay him, nor even of those who can not. No other business man does it, and he is going to quit it, too.

In the midst of his meditations comes that ever-recurring knock at the door. The doctor goes, a little impatiently, to open it. His wife hears the conversation. It is an appealing call for him to go down into the country seven or eight miles to see a very sick woman, the wife of the man at the door. The doctor is strong in his new resolution, and says, sternly, "No, sir; I have gone down to your house often enough without getting anything for it."

The man outside is amazed into silence. He stands speechless a moment; then says, "I know it, Doc., and I'm ashamed of it; but it ain't her fault. She's always done her part."

"I'm sorry for her; but I've got my own family to work for, and I am not going to work for you any longer for nothing. If you have the money to pay me to-night, I will go."

"I hain't got it, Doc., and I can't git it to-night."

"If you don't pay it to-night, you never will pay it; so you can go and get somebody else."

"Nobody else will go, either, without the money—and—she's awful sick, Doc.; won't you go this time if I'll promise to pay you next week, sure?"

"No, sir."

The door is closed, the man goes with slow and undecided steps away, and the doctor comes back to his chair. He tries to look unconcerned and as if he knew he had done the right thing; but it is an effort, and husband and wife both know it, though neither of them speak of it. The husband picks up a paper, and the wife at the window looks out into the moonlight and thinks of the poor woman, who has always done her part, who lies sick and unattended now because of one who has not done his part. She has often told the doctor he was wearing himself out for other people who would not lift a hand to help him if help were needed; she thinks, of course, that he has done right in refusing to go; and yet—and yet—

The doctor does not rest well this night. It is a long while before he gets to sleep. Early in the morning, before day has fairly dawned, the wife awakes, to find him up and nearly dressed.

"I guess I'd better go down there. I won't feel easy till I do."

And somehow the wife has no inclination, in this instance, to remind him that he is wearing himself out for nothing. The sick wife who had always done her part had lingered in her thoughts, too, last night, and she is glad of the doctor's compassion. He is soon on his way. Let us follow him in fancy and drink in deep draughts of the fresh morning air and see the sun rise over the hills. How glorious is early morning in the country! How dark and cool is this belt of woodland, this remnant of a "dim old forest" through which we are passing now! And how peaceful and sweet the dew-bathed meadows beyond! The "drowsy tinklings" of the bells of cattle which last night "lulled the distant fold" are animated tinklings now; the birds are singing in an ecstasy of joy, and all the world is waking.

THE PHYSICIAN'S WIFE.

Surely an hour and a scene like this have an uplifting power upon the doctor's spirit; for see how rapidly he drives! By and by he stops before a very poor little house. No one is in sight. He ties his horse, steps over the low, tumble-down rail-fence, and walks up to the door.

Enter softly, Doctor!

> "There's one in that poor shed,
> One by that lowly bed,
> Greater than thou!"

No one has sent for him; no one has seen him come. But he is there. His compassion is infinitely greater than thine, Doctor. You put a price upon your coming last night; he came without money and without price. If it were possible now, you would raise that stricken form  and set those feet once more in the thorny paths of life. He knows how weary grew the feet,

and he will lead them into green pastures and
beside still waters, where at last they may find
rest. Yes; pitying Death has come before you,
and in one moment more will claim his own.
And does the doctor find consolation in the
thought, as many others might do, that here is
one more weary life of poverty and toil and abuse
ended, and that it is better so? Ah, no; it was
her life, and to it, perhaps, she clung as tena-
ciously as the queen in her palace. He knows
that, whatever others may think and feel in
times like this, his mission, his sympathies, his
work must be on the side of life, and not of
death. However great the deliverance death
may bring, it is not his to hasten it, in an infini-
tesimal degree, by aught that he may do or leave
undone. It is vain for him to reason that his
coming last night would, perhaps, have made no
difference. He had a chance to do something
toward saving this fellow-being's life, and he did
it not. He had a chance, if not to save a life, at
least to alleviate suffering, and he did it not.
His thoughts go back to the days of his youth

and early manhood, when, full of enthusiasm in his chosen profession, he had started out with his heart running high with hope, and the wish to do something good in the world, and had flung his banner proudly to the breezes. The advancing years, with the burdens which the years inevitably bring, had many times brought that banner low, but he feels that it has never trailed so utterly in the dust as it did last night. And as he stands, with bowed head, and looks down into the dying eyes, they seem to say to his remorseful heart, " I was so sick, and you visited me not"; and then, far off through the centuries, comes a holy voice, " Inasmuch as ye have done it unto one of the least of these, ye have done it unto Me." And he did it not.

You and I, reader, have followed the doctor only in fancy to this dying bed, yet I beg to assure you this is no fancy sketch. It is drawn from life, and is, perhaps, only one of many similar instances. Though many years have gone by since that scene at early morning, the doctor does not forget it. It is not hard to see that, in the presence of things like this, the physician's resolutions to work only for himself and his family must vanish away, and that, in the future as in the past, much of his work, his time, and his strength must be given where they will bring him little or nothing in return.

And therefore the physician's wife, pondering these things in her heart,—thinking of the countless deeds of kindness and mercy he has been doing through all these years in the name of charity, sweet charity,—thinks within herself that if, in a better world than this, there is a crown a little more radiant than all the rest, surely it must be waiting for the physician's brow.

We, their wives, cannot do the good in the world that our husbands have it in their power to do. Our sphere is circumscribed; and so our real usefulness to those around us, as compared

with theirs, may be likened, perhaps, as shadow
unto form. But it is good to know that shadows,
too, have had their mission in the world. The
wounded and dying soldiers in that Crimean
hospital, who turned upon their beds to kiss the
shadow of saintly Florence Nightingale as it fell
upon them, have told us that. To them it was
a holy shadow.

There is an old French legend which, because it contains a lesson for us all, I will give,
in part:—

A long time ago there lived a saint so good
that the angels, astonished at his holiness, came
expressly from heaven to see how any one on
earth could so closely resemble the good God.
Two words summed up his day. He *gave* and
forgave, but these words were never on his lips;
you read them in his smile, in his amiability, in
his courtesy, in his untiring charity. The angels
said to God, "Lord, grant him the gift of miracle." "Willingly," replied the good God. "Ask
him what he wishes." But the saint wished for
nothing. In reply to all their questions as to

whether he would choose this gift or that, he only answered "No." The angels insisted, saying, "Nevertheless, you must ask a miracle." Then, said the saint, "Let me do a great deal of good in the world without ever knowing it."

The angels consulted together for some time how this could be accomplished; then they asked the good God to grant that every time the saint's shadow fell at either side or behind him so that he could not see it it should have the power of healing the sick, consoling the afflicted, and comforting the sorrowful. Our Lord assented. And wherever the saint's shadow fell thus the pathways bloomed, the turbid streams became pure and limpid, a fresh bloom came to the cheeks of little children, and tears of joy to the eyes of sorrowing mothers.

But the saint kept simply on his way, unconsciously spreading the example of his virtues as the stars shed light, as the flowers give perfume.

And the people, respecting his modesty, followed him in silence, never speaking to him of his miracles. They gradually forgot even his name, and simply called him "The Holy Shadow."

It is thus that we may work. Quietly, unostentatiously, carrying with us into the sick-room, or anywhere else, the cheerful heart, which wise old Solomon has told us doeth good like a medicine. Speaking the word, as occasion may sometimes present, which, fitly spoken, is like apples of gold in pictures of silver. The time has never come to me when a word of honest appreciation or regard has not touched an answering chord.

Be assured it does not come to others either, and withhold nothing of happiness it is in your power to bestow.

We shall realize, of course, as the years go by, that we cannot do all that we might wish to do; cannot have all that we most wish to have; for wishing and having have evermore been widely sundered; but, like the saint of the legend, if we keep simply on our way, doing the little that we may in this world,—

> "It may be, when all is done,
> We shall be together in some good world,
> Where to wish and to have are one."

Recently Issued.

Consumption: ✳ ✳
✳ ✳ How to Prevent it and How to Live with it.

Its Nature, Causes, Prevention, and the Mode of Life, Climate, Exercise, Food, and Clothing Necessary for its Cure.

BY

N. S. DAVIS, Jr., A.M., M.D.,

Professor of Principles and Practice of Medicine, Chicago Medical College; Physician to Mercy Hospital, Chicago; Member of the American Medical Association, etc., etc.

THIS is a plain, practical treatise, thoroughly readable and scientifically accurate; written by one of the best-qualified physicians in the United States. The most reliable information is given in this volume respecting the Prevention of Consumption, Hygiene for Consumptives, timely suggestions concerning the different climates and the important part they play in the treatment of this disease, etc., etc., all presented in such a succinct and intelligible style as to make the perusal of the book a pleasant pastime. Many thousands, more or less affected by this fearful scourge, would be truly benefited by enforcing the principles and methods outlined and largely elaborated in this handy volume.

In one neat 12mo volume of 143 pages. Handsomely Bound in Extra Cloth, with Back and Side Stamps in Gold. Price, post-paid, 75 cents net.

THE F. A. DAVIS COMPANY, Publishers,
1914 and 1916 Cherry Street,
PHILADELPHIA, PA.

SIXTH THOUSAND NOW READY.

An Important Book for the Family and School.

CHILDHOOD.
MAIDENHOOD.
WIFEHOOD.
MOTHERHOOD.

THE DAUGHTER:

Her Health, Education, and Wedlock.

By **WILLIAM M. CAPP, M.D.**, Philadelphia.

IT is thoughtful and suggestive on subjects affecting woman's highest interests in domestic life, and in style is dignified and earnest, refined and modest. Health, education, sexual development, courtship, betrothal, marriage, maternity, and related subjects are comprehensively treated in a manner which charms by its delicacy and high moral tone. It does not pander to corrupt tastes or prurient curiosity, as works on these themes too often do. It teaches what every mother should know and impart to her daughter. It is a book for physicians to recommend to lady patients, and should be at hand for reference in every family and school. BEAUTIFULLY PRINTED IN LARGE, CLEAR TYPE. 12MO. 150 PAGES. NEATLY BOUND IN EXTRA CLOTH.

Price, post-paid, $1.00 net. Also bound in Paper Covers (unabridged), 50 cents net.

AN ATTRACTIVE AND USEFUL GIFT.

Few books have ever been so UNANIMOUSLY recommended by the literary, religious, and scientific press, and physicians of eminence everywhere. Send for circular giving reviews and criticisms.

THE F. A. DAVIS COMPANY, PUBLISHERS,
1914 AND 1916 CHERRY ST., PHILA., PA.

www.ingramcontent.com/pod-product-compliance
Lightning Source LLC
Chambersburg PA
CBHW020926230426
43666CB00008B/1587